The Hermetica

Also by Timothy Freke

Tao Te Ching

Also by Timothy Freke and Peter Gandy

The Complete Guide to World Mysticism

The Hermetica
The Lost Wisdom of the Pharaohs

Timothy Freke and Peter Gandy

Jeremy P. Tarcher/Putnam
a member of
Penguin Putnam Inc.
New York

To the memory of
Giordano Bruno,
1548–1600

Mundus Nihil Pulcherrimum
The World Is a Beautiful Nothing

Most Tarcher/Putnam books are available at special quantity
discounts for bulk purchases for sales promotions, premiums,
fund-raising, and educational needs. Special books or book
excerpts also can be created to fit specific needs. For details,
write Putnam Special Markets, 375 Hudson Street, New York,
NY 10014.

Jeremy P. Tarcher/Putnam
a member of
Penguin Putnam Inc.
375 Hudson Street
New York, NY 10014
www.penguinputnam.com

First published in 1997 by Judy Piatkus Ltd, 5 Windmill Street,
London W1P 1HF

Library of Congress Cataloging-in-Publication Data

Freke, Timothy, date.
    The hermetica: the lost wisdom of the pharaohs / Timothy
Freke and Peter Gandy.
        p.   cm.
    Originally published: London: Judy Piatkus Publishers, 1997.
    Includes bibliographical references.
    ISBN 0-87477-950-2
    1. Hermeticism.   I. Gandy, Peter.   II. Hermes,
Trismegistus.   Corpus Hermeticum.   III. Title.
BF1601.F74   1998   98-39902   CIP
135'.45—dc21

Book design by Zena Flax
Cover design by Allan Spain

Printed in the United States of America
        3   4   5   6   7   8   9   10

This book is printed on acid-free paper. ⊚

Contents

The Last Words of
Thrice-Great Hermes

'Wise words,
although written
by my decaying hand,
remain imperishable
through time;
Imbued with the medicine
of immortality
by the All-Master.
Be unseen
and undiscovered
by all those
who will come and go,
wandering
the wastelands of life.
Be hidden,
until an older heaven
births human beings
who are worthy
of your wisdom.'

Having sounded this prayer
over the works of his hands,
Hermes was received
in the sanctuary of eternity.

Introduction

A Forgotten Spiritual Classic

The Hermetica is a collection of writings attributed to Thoth – a mythical ancient Egyptian sage whose wisdom is said to have transformed him into a god. Thoth, who was venerated in Egypt from at least 3000 BCE, is credited with the invention of sacred hieroglyphic writing, and his figure, portrayed as a scribe with the head of an ibis, can be seen in many temples and tombs. He is the dispatcher of divine messages and recorder of all human deeds. In the Great Hall of Judgment, the after-life court of the god Osiris, Thoth would establish whether the deceased had acquired spiritual knowledge and purity, and so deserved a place in the heavens. Thoth was said to have revealed to the Egyptians all knowledge on astronomy, architecture, geometry, medicine and religion, and was believed by the ancient Greeks to be the architect of the pyramids. The Greeks, who were in awe of the knowledge and spirituality of the Egyptians, identified Thoth with their own god Hermes, the messenger of the gods and guider of souls in the realm of the dead. To distinguish the Egyptian Hermes from their own, they gave him the title 'Trismegistus', meaning 'Thrice-Great', to honour his sublime wisdom. The books attributed to him became collectively known as the 'Hermetica'.

Although largely unknown today, the writings attributed to Hermes/Thoth have been immensely important in the history of Western thought. They profoundly influenced the Greeks and, through their rediscovery in fifteenth-century Florence, helped to inspire the 'Renaissance' which gave birth to our modern age. The list of people who have acknowledged a debt to the Hermetica reads like a 'Who's Who' of the greatest philosophers, scientists and artists that the West has produced – Leonardo da Vinci, Dürer, Botticelli, Roger Bacon, Paracelsus, Thomas More, William Blake, Kepler, Copernicus, Isaac Newton, Sir Walter Raleigh, Milton, Ben Johnson, Daniel Defoe, Shelley and his wife Mary, Victor Hugo and Carl Jung. It heavily influenced Shakespeare, John Donne, John Dee and all the poet-philosophers who surrounded the court of Queen Elizabeth I, as well as the founding scientists of the Royal Society in London, and even the leaders who inspired the Protestant Reformation in Europe. The list is endless, with the Hermetica's influence reaching well beyond the frontiers of Europe. Islamic mystics and philosophers also trace their inspiration back to Thrice-Great Hermes, and the esoteric tradition of the Jews equated him with their mysterious prophet Enoch.

The Hermetica is a cornerstone of Western culture. In substance and importance it is equal to well-known Eastern scriptures like the Upanishads, the Dhammapada and the Tao Te Ching. Yet, unlike these texts which are now readily available and widely read, the works of Hermes have been lost under the dead weight of academic translations, Christian prejudice and occult obscurities. Until now, no simplified rendering of these writings has been available to the general reader. All previous versions in the English language are very dense, impenetrable, and loaded down with notes and subtext that make them difficult to digest. This new version, however, makes this ancient wisdom more easily accessible. It presents carefully selected extracts of the Hermetic texts, linked together into a narrative and rendered into easily understood English. What emerges is an inspiring and illuminating taste of a forgotten classic.

Introduction

The History of the Hermetica

The early origins of the Hermetica are shrouded in mystery, but the evidence suggests it is a direct descendant of the ancient philosophy of the Egyptians. However, the handful of surviving works attributed to Hermes are not written in ancient Egyptian hieroglyphs, but in Greek, Latin and Coptic. They were collated in the city of Alexandria in Egypt during the second and third centuries CE. Here the Hermetic philosophy helped inspire some of the greatest intellectual achievements of the ancient world. Alexandria was a great centre of learning, surpassing even Athens. Its founder, Alexander the Great, had conquered and united Greece, Persia, Egypt and India into one vast empire. Cultures that had grown up more or less independently were brought together, and there was no bigger melting pot than Alexandria. Into this new 'Universal City' (Gk. *cosmos-polis*), poured men and women of every race and nation. Greeks, Jews, Egyptians, Babylonians, Phoenicians and even Buddhists from India associated together in relative peace.

The Alexandrians were renowned for their thirst for knowledge, and under the enlightened Greek ruler Ptolemy I a library and museum were founded where human beings first systematically collected the wisdom of the world. At its height, the library of Alexandria housed some half a million scrolls. These included the works of Euclid, Archimedes and the astronomer Ptolemy, who dominated the spheres of geometry, mathematics and geography respectively until well into the Middle Ages. It contained the research of Aristarchus of Samos, who had shown that the Earth is one of the planets orbiting the sun, and Eratosthenes, who had calculated the circumference of the Earth to within a few per cent. Scientists of the library knew about the precession of the equinoxes and that the moon was responsible for the rhythm of the tides. Alexandria was also rich in esoteric knowledge – Pythagorism, Chaldean oracles, Greek myths, Platonic and Stoic philosophy, Judaism, Christianity, the Greek Mystery Schools, Zoroastrianism, astrology, alchemy, Buddhism and of course the ancient Egyptian religion were all practised, studied, compared and discussed.

The golden age of Alexandria came to an end with the birth of the intolerant Christian 'Holy' Roman Empire. Despite the sophistication and cultural achievements of the ancients, the Christians referred to them dismissively as 'Pagans', which means 'country-dwellers'. In 415 CE, Hypatia, one of the last great scientists and Pagan philosophers working at the library of Alexandria, was seized by a mob of Christians, who removed her flesh with scallop shells and burnt her remains. Their leader, Bishop Cyril, was later canonised St Cyril. The great library was finally destroyed as so much Pagan superstition, and this wealth of knowledge was scattered to the four winds. The Christian Roman Emperor Theodosius closed Pagan temples across the empire and began the previously unknown phenomenon of book-burning. For the West, the fifth century ushered in the thousand-year period appropriately known as the Dark Ages.

The Hermetica and Islam

History shows that wherever the works of Hermes have been studied and venerated, civilisation has flourished. Pagan scholars and sages fled to the newly emerging Arab culture, taking their knowledge and the Hermetic writings with them. Two hundred years later, the Muslims created an empire whose learning and scientific achievements were unsurpassed. By the beginning of the ninth century, the first university was established in Baghdad, called the 'House of Wisdom'. Here many Pagan works were translated, the sciences that had reached such heights in

Alexandria were significantly developed, and the ancient Pagan spiritual wisdom was covertly studied and practised. From its exalted position amongst the sacred scriptures of Egyptian spirituality, the Hermetica became the secret inspiration for an important undercurrent in Islamic philosophy, and the holy book of unorthodox religious sects such as the Sabaeans.

We would never have heard of the mysterious Sabaeans had they not come into conflict with the religious authorities of their day. Several centuries after the death of its founder, Muhammad, Islam was beginning to succumb to the same desire for orthodoxy that had arisen in the Christian West. Heretics were to be rooted out – if necessary with violence. In 830 CE a powerful Caliph was passing through the city of Harran when he noticed the strangely dressed Sabaeans and questioned their leaders. Asked to produce their sacred texts, they returned with the books of Hermes. The genius philosopher–scientist Thabbit Ibn Qurra was a Sabaean who in 810 CE wrote the following rousing defence of Hermetic Paganism:

> We are the heirs and propagators of Paganism.
> Happy is he who for the sake of Paganism bears
> the burden of persecution with firm hope. Who
> else have civilised the world and built cities if
> not the nobles and kings of Paganism? Who else
> have set in order the harbours and the rivers?
> And who else have taught the hidden wisdom?
> To whom else has the Deity revealed itself,
> given oracles, and told about the future, if not
> the famous men amongst the Pagans? The
> Pagans have made known all of this. They have
> discovered the art of healing the body, they
> have also made known the art of healing the
> soul; they have filled the earth with settled
> forms of government and with wisdom which is

the highest good. Without Paganism the world
would be empty and miserable.

Thabbit Ibn Qurra

Another unorthodox group within the Islamic empire who
also traced their ancestry back to Thrice-Great Hermes were
the poets and mystics known as the Sufis. The twelfth-
century Iranian Sufi philosopher Yahya Suhrawardi made it
his life's work to link what he called the 'original oriental
religion' with Islam. He claimed that the sages of the ancient
world had preached a single doctrine. This had been
originally revealed to Hermes, whom Suhrawardi identified
with the prophet known as 'Idris' in the Koran and the
Jewish prophet 'Enoch'. In the Greek world, he claimed,
this philosophy had been transmitted through Pythagoras
and Plato, and in the Middle East through the Zoroastrian
Magi. It had been secretly passed on until it had reached
himself through a direct line of enlightened sages including
his own master the Sufi mystic Al Hallaj. Not surprisingly
both Suhrawardi and Al Hallaj were executed by the
religious authorities for heresy – Al Hallaj by crucifixion.

Hermes and the Reawakening of Europe

With the Arab empire becoming increasingly intolerant, the
owners of the Hermetic books travelled in search of a safe
refuge. In the fifteenth century many fled to the tolerant
city-state of Florence in Northern Italy, where this wisdom
again inspired a great cultural flowering. In 1438 the
Byzantine scholar Gemisto Plethon made available to the
awe-struck Florentines the entire lost works of Plato. These
and other Pagan works were translated into Latin for the
first time. The ruler of Florence, the philanthropist and
scholar Cosimo de' Medici, established a New Platonic
Academy – a group of intellectuals and mystics who found

their inspiration in the ancient Pagan philosophy. It profoundly influenced great names like Leonardo da Vinci, Michelangelo, Botticelli and Raphael, who began painting pictures of the ancient Pagan gods. Botticelli's 'Venus and Mars', for example, was painted at a precise astrological moment as a 'talisman of occult radiance', capable of magically transporting the viewer to an altered state of spiritual awareness.

Cosimo sent out agents to look for other lost Pagan works that might still be awaiting discovery. In 1460 one of them came across the lost works of Thrice-Great Hermes, and brought them to Florence. The Florentines, already reeling from the discovery that an ancient civilisation of immense sophistication had risen and fallen nearly 2000 years before them, now believed they had in their hands the words of the most ancient sage of them all. Cosimo ordered his young Greek scholar Marsilio Ficino to cease his work on translating Plato and to begin immediately on this new Egyptian text. Ficino had it ready in time to read to Cosimo just before his death.

The emergence of a glorious new culture in Florence signalled the end of the Dark Ages. We call this period the 'Renaissance', meaning 'rebirth', which is a fitting name, for at the heart of the Hermetic philosophy is the idea of being spiritually reborn. The ancient Pagan wisdom arrived in Florence at a fortuitous moment in history. Within a few years the first printing presses arrived in Italy and the Pagan wisdom was printed and dispersed throughout Europe. Students of the 'New Learning', as the Florentine experiment became known, were sent out as emissaries, beginning new movements wherever they went.

Reuchlin, 'the father of the Reformation' and teacher of Luther and Erasmus, left Florence and sowed the earliest seeds of the Protestant Reformation in Germany. Thomas Linacre founded the Royal College of Physicians in London. The mathematician Nicholas of Cusa, the physician

Paracelsus, the architect Brunelleschi and the astronomer Toscanelli (whose famous map inspired Christopher Columbus) all owed their inspiration to the Florentine reawakening of the spirit of ancient Paganism. Copernicus' momentous claim that the sun, not the Earth, is at the centre of the solar system was a choice, not a discovery, made after studying Hermetic/Platonic philosophy at an Italian university. On the first page of *On the Revolution of the Celestial Orbs*, published in 1543, Copernicus quotes the words of Thrice-Great Hermes – 'The Sun is the Visible God'.

As in Alexandria a thousand years earlier, the Renaissance viewed science, art, literature and religion as parts of a united whole to be studied together. All aspects of human life were now opened up as legitimate areas of investigation. It was a situation that challenged the authorities of the Roman Catholic Church and in 1492, with the aid of the King of France, they crushed the Republic of Florence. Although the heady days of the New Academy were over, the suppression was too late to prevent the ripples of its influence expanding ever outwards. Florentine scholars were dispersed across Europe and became known as the 'Fifth Essence'. The taste for all things Italian – art, sculpture, fashion, literature and philosophy – was insatiable. Within less than 200 years, the Renaissance had conquered Europe.

The Unifying Religion

In England the works of Hermes had a profound effect on the circle of courtiers surrounding Elizabeth I. Sir Philip Sydney, Sir Walter Raleigh, John Donne, Christopher Marlowe, William Shakespeare, George Chapman, and Francis Bacon were all acquainted with the works of the Egyptian sage. Elizabeth's personal astrologer, whom she

referred to as 'her philosopher', was the enigmatic
Hermeticist John Dee. He was a brilliant mathematician and
the first person to translate the complete works of Euclid
into English. Doctor Dee owned the greatest library in
England and his home was regarded as a third university to
Oxford and Cambridge. He was visited by scholars from all
over Europe and made frequent journeys to Prague where
the first detailed commentaries on the Hermetica were
being written. At this time Prague was the capital of
Bohemia, an enlightened republic where Hermetic scholars,
Platonic philosophers, Jewish rabbis, and scientists of every
nation found sanctuary at the court of Rudolph II. Europe
was being ravaged by the Wars of Religion between
Protestants and Catholics, and in Bohemia another way was
proposed – Hermeticism.

Evangelists of the new 'Egyptian' religion of Thrice-
Great Hermes, such as Giordano Bruno, travelled
extensively in Europe. Bruno interpreted the new sun-
centred cosmos proposed by Copernicus in an entirely
mystical way, as the rising of a new sun at the dawning of a
New Age. He believed that the Egyptian religion of Hermes
was the ancestor of the Greek Mystery Schools, the religion
of Moses and the Jews, and the birthplace of Christianity. In
Bruno's imagination it was now poised to become the
unifying religion in which Jews, all denominations of
Christians, Platonic humanists, and even Muslims could
meet and resolve their differences. Bruno's courage and
conviction was nowhere more clearly demonstrated than in
his decision to return to Italy, where within a short time he
was arrested by the Roman Catholic Church. He endured
eight years of torture during which he refused to recant,
and in 1600 was led out into the 'Square of Flowers' in
Rome and ceremonially burnt alive.

The vision of a universal Hermetic religion was fated
to fade, but its influence remained strong amongst
visionaries and scientists. Sir Isaac Newton, for example,

like many men of his time, was passionately interested in alchemy, the patron god of which was Thrice-Great Hermes. Indeed the word 'alchemy' means 'from Egypt'. The astronomer Kepler published quotes from the Hermetica in his greatest work, *On the Harmony of the World*. In 1640 the poet John Milton celebrated the wisdom of Hermes, writing:

> Or let my lamp at midnight hour
> Be seen in some high lonely tower,
> Where I may oft outwatch the Bear
> With Thrice-Great Hermes, or unsphere
> The spirit of Plato, to unfold
> What worlds, or what vast regions hold
> The immortal Mind that hath forsook
> Her mansion in this fleshy nook.
>
> *Il Penseroso*

The Demise of Thrice-Great Hermes

At the same time as Milton was writing, however, the ground was being cut away from under the authenticity of the Hermetica. Previously these works had been believed to be of extreme antiquity – dating back to the time of the pharaohs. In 1614 a scholar called Isaac Casaubon published a textual analysis of the Hermetica, which showed, quite correctly, that the grammar, vocabulary, form and content of the Greek versions of these works dated them to no earlier than the second and third centuries CE. They were not written by an ancient Egyptian sage, he claimed, but by scholars in the city of Alexandria. Their philosophy was nothing more than an exotic blend of Greek, Christian and Jewish philosophy, mixed up with astrology and magic. The Egyptian names that pepper the text were mere decoration and ornament. Casaubon was one of the most brilliant Greek scholars of his time and, with the encouragement of the Christian status quo, his damning criticism was generally accepted. Casaubon had dealt the Egyptian sage a fatal blow, and the books of Hermes were destined to be forgotten as fakes and forgeries.

In the modern world we know from the actions of the tabloid press how one well-timed 'hatchet job' can unjustifiably undermine someone's reputation for good. This is exactly what happened to Thrice-Great Hermes. Casaubon was a fine scholar, but he was motivated by a hidden political agenda. The ultra-orthodox James I was now on the throne of England and he employed Casaubon and others to purge the magically inclined court of Elizabeth. Hermeticists like John Dee were ostracized. Later, Casaubon's son Merick wrote a book which portrayed the great philosopher as a confused occultist. Dee died alone and forgotten.

Nonetheless some of Casaubon's claims regarding the Hermetica are true. The Books of Hermes are undoubtedly the products of many authors, not one ancient sage, and they were certainly composed in the first few centuries of our era. Hermes was credited with these writings, even though we know they were the composite work of many scholars, but this does not discredit either them or Hermes. It was a common practice in antiquity for authors to ascribe their work to the god who gave them their inspiration. This was a mark of respect, not an attempt to deceive. On the second charge, Casaubon is also right to claim that the Hermetica was written down in second-century Alexandria, but all the modern evidence suggests that it does in fact express Egyptian beliefs filtered through the understanding of the Greek scholars of the period. Even if all Casaubon's criticisms were correct, this would neither diminish the Hermetica's wisdom, nor alter the fact that it has profoundly influenced some of the greatest minds in history. As old as the Christian gospels and older than the Koran, it is one of the great sacred texts of the world. It is worthy of respect and study for these reasons alone.

The Wisdom of the Pharaohs

When Casaubon was writing, very little was actually known about ancient Egypt. The hieroglyphs themselves were not translated until two centuries after his death. Consequently many modern scholars now believe that he was wrong to see the Hermetic philosophy as a second-century invention, especially since the discovery of the pyramid texts of Saqquara at the end of the last century. These hieroglyphs are over 5000 years old and yet contain doctrines that are identical to those expounded in the Hermetica.

This suggests that the Hermetica may indeed contain the wisdom of the pharaohs, which scholars in second-century Alexandria reworked for a contemporary readership.

The Hermetica contains passages reminiscent of Jewish, Christian, and Greek works, and Casaubon saw this as proof that the Hermetica is a forgery, created from a hotchpotch of these other philosophies. Alexandria was such an eclectic environment that this is plausible. The ancients themselves believed, however, that these traditions were influenced by the Egyptian philosophy contained within the Hermetica. The Jews lived for many years in exile in Egypt and their greatest prophet Moses was brought up as an Egyptian; many early Christians lived in Egypt; and the Greeks were in awe of the Egyptians, compared to whom they felt like children. The ancient Greek historian Herodotus writes:

> The Egyptians are religious to excess, beyond
> any other nation in the world . . . they are
> meticulous in everything which concerns their

> religion . . . It was only, if I may put it so, the
> day before yesterday that the Greeks came to
> know the origin and form of the various gods
> . . . The names of all the gods came to Greece
> from Egypt . . . for the names of all the gods
> have been known in Egypt from the beginning
> of time.
>
> *Herodotus*

Casaubon particularly claims that the Hermetica plagiarised the Timaeus – a work written by the Greek philosopher Plato in the fifth century BCE. Like the Hermetica, it includes the doctrines of astrology and reincarnation. Yet, these ideas played no part in early Greek religion, so where did they come from? The answer is ancient Egypt. Over a hundred years before Plato, the Greek sage Pythagoras had set out on a journey to acquire the knowledge of the world. This led him to Egypt where he spent twenty-two years in the temples being initiated into the religion of the Egyptians. According to the ancient Greek scholar Diogenes Laertius, Plato purchased three books of Pythagorean doctrines based on Egyptian wisdom, and these he adapted into the Timaeus. The similarities between the works of Plato and the Hermetica are not surprising, therefore, since many of Plato's ideas were direct descendants of ancient Egyptian philosophy.

The Hermetica and Early Christianity

Hermetic philosophy also influenced Christianity through the Alexandrian church fathers St Clement and St Origen, who synthesised Pagan and Christian religious doctrines. It is due to such theologians that the Hermetic concept of 'The Word' is found in the opening verse of the Gospel of John: 'In the beginning was the Word'. Hermes/Thoth was known to the ancients as the scribe of the gods and master of 'The Word'. In the Hermetica, God utters a Word which calms the chaotic waters of creation. The Word is even called the 'Son of God'. In Christianity Jesus Christ, who is also called 'The Son of God', is identified as an embodiment of the power of the 'Word'. St Augustine of Hippo, the influential fourth-century theologian who was familiar with the works of Hermes, writes:

> That which is called the Christian religion
> existed among the ancients, and never did not
> exist, from the beginning of the human race
> until Christ came in the flesh, at which time the
> true religion which already existed began to be
> called Christianity.
>
> *St Augustine, Retractions*

The influence of the Hermetica on early Christianity is beyond doubt. In 1945 works of Hermes were discovered amongst scriptures belonging to Gnostic Christians of the first centuries CE. According to a note on one of the texts, early Christian communities possessed many copies of the works of Hermes. Just a few yards from the place where these scriptures were found are ancient Egyptian tombs. These were inhabited by early Christian hermits, such as St Pachomius, the founder of the first Christian monastic communities. The walls of these tombs are covered in hieroglyphs ascribed to the great god Thoth (Hermes). They describe a spiritual rebirth into knowledge of God. In such places early Gnostic Christians pored over the Hermetica. Under its powerful influence, they composed their own philosophy of a saving *Gnosis* (Gk. 'knowledge') – a direct knowledge of God bestowed by the messiah Jesus.

All the evidence suggests that Casaubon was wrong to simply dismiss the Hermetica as some cobbled-together mixture of many different philosophies. The Hermetica was undoubtedly written by Alexandrian scholars for a Greek-speaking readership. But it contains a powerful echo of the ancient wisdom on which it was based. It offers us one of the best windows available to gaze into Egypt's remotest past. With its help we can understand the mystical vision that inspired the awesome Giza pyramids. But what is the Hermetic philosophy that has held such a profound fascination for some of the greatest minds in history?

The Mind of God

At the heart of Hermes' teachings is one simple idea – God is a Big Mind. Everything which exists is a thought within the Mind of God. This book is a thought in the Mind of God. Your body is a thought in the Mind of God. These ideas which are being discussed are thoughts in the Mind of God. How can we understand this?

Consider for a moment your own experience. Thoughts and feelings exist within your mind. You know the outer world around you because your senses give you information which you also then experience within your mind. When your mind is completely unconscious, you don't experience anything. Ultimately, everything that exists in your life is a thought within your mind. Your mind, however, is limited by being trapped in a physical body. Imagine for a moment that it is not. Imagine that it is free to be conscious of everything, at all times and in all places. Then everything that is, has been, and will be, would exist as a thought within your mind. This is the nature of God's Mind. He is not limited by a physical body. He is the Big Mind within which everything exists.

Hermes describes the Mind of God as the Oneness which unites everything. What does this mean? Again, look at your own experience. You experience many different things with your mind. Right now you are reading this book. Before that you may have been eating, or walking in the country. Yet all of these different things are experienced by one thing – your mind. It is the Oneness that unites all of your experience. In the same way, God's Mind is the Oneness which unites everything.

Hermes says that this Oneness contains all opposites. This paradox can be understood by once more looking at the nature of your own mind. Some things you experience are hot and others cold; some are bright and others dark; some you call good and others bad. Nothing that you experience can be both cold and hot, because they are opposites. Yet both cold and hot are experiences which you have. Your mind is the one thing which contains all opposites.

Hermes teaches that the mind of a human being is made in the image of God's Big Mind. If we can free our mind from the limitations imposed by the physical body, we can experience the Mind of God. We were created with the specific purpose of learning to do this. This is the spiritual goal of human life. To reach this destination we must expand our awareness. We must use the power of our little minds to reach out to God's Big Mind.

To help us do this, Hermes narrates a dramatic story of how God creates and maintains the cosmos. It is through appreciating the awesome beauty of the cosmos and understanding the fundamental laws by which it functions, that we can come to know the Mind of God. It was this vision which fired the imaginations of the great minds of history. It inspired the birth of science by encouraging them to explore the Mind of God by seeking to discover more of how the universe works. Some great modern scientists, such as Albert Einstein and Stephen Hawking, still describe science as an attempt to understand 'the Mind of God'. The Hermetic philosophy places man at the very centre of God's creation. Hermes declares that 'man is a marvel'. With his mind he may not only understand the universe, but even come to know God. He is not a mortal body which will live and die. He is an immortal soul which, through the experience of a spiritual rebirth, may become a god.

A New Version of the Hermetica

A book of this size cannot contain all the Hermetic teachings. It can, however, give an inspirational and intriguing taste of their core doctrines. The main surviving philosophical Hermetic texts are the eighteen books known as the Corpus Hermeticum (seventeen survive, Book XV is missing), the Asclepius, the Stobaeus and various fragments. These works are dense and somewhat impenetrable. In this new version, therefore, we have selected key extracts and combined them to bring out the essential wisdom and inherent poetry that they contain. In this endeavour we feel we are following in the footsteps of the scholars of Alexandria who collated these books from the ancient material that was then available, making them accessible to a contemporary readership. Our sources are contained in notes at the back of the book, but for most readers it will be enough to follow a progressive exposition of the essence of Hermeticism, condensed into more manageable sections.

Like many Greek texts, the Hermetic teachings are often presented in the form of dialogues between teacher and pupil. The voices change in the different texts, which can be confusing, so we have chosen to avoid this device and simply present a monologue by Hermes addressed to the reader. Although we have used the familiar term 'God' in the explanatory notes which accompany each chapter, we have avoided this term in the text itself. Instead we have used 'Atum' – one of the ancient Egyptian names for the Supreme One-God. We felt that using this unfamiliar Egyptian name would allow the reader the opportunity to build up their own conceptual picture of what Hermes means by the term, free of any associations they may have with the word 'God'.

It is a daunting task to present a new version of any work that is written in a foreign language and uses a distinct and unique conceptual vocabulary. Approaching a text which is also of extreme antiquity and has already been through the hands of a number of translators is doubly difficult. In Book XVI of the Corpus Hermeticum, Hermes writes:

> My teachings will seem more obscure
> in times to come,
> when they are translated
> from our Egyptian mother tongue
> into that of the Greeks.
> Translation will distort much of their meaning.
> Expressed in our native language,
> the teachings are clear and simple,
> for the very sound of an Egyptian word
> resonates with the thing signified by it.
> All possible measures should be taken
> to prevent these holy secrets being corrupted
> by translation into Greek,
> which is an arrogant, feeble, showy language,
> unable to contain the cogent force of my words.
> The Greek language lacks the power to convince,
> and Greek philosophy is nothing but noisy chatter.
> Our Egyptian speech is more than talk.
> Its utterances are replete with power.

In the ancient Egyptian language the sound of a word had a magical power which complemented its meaning – a view of language which we unconsciously retain when we talk of 'spelling' a word. Translation inevitably means that we have lost this original power and clarity. Hermes teaches, however, that through the power of the mind all things are possible. We have tried, through the power of contemplation which Hermes advocates, to distil the essence of his teachings for a new generation of spiritual seekers.

Although human culture has changed beyond recognition from the times of the ancient Egyptians, the essential mysteries of life have remained what they have always been and always will be. For those alive to these mysteries, the writings of Hermes are as relevant today as they were in the distant past. We hope this new version captures as much as possible of the Hermetic vision, playing some small part in restoring to this ancient wisdom the respect that it is due.

I. The Prophecies of Hermes

In this chapter Hermes describes the nature of pure philosophy, but laments that in future generations it will become all but lost.

The philosophy that Hermes teaches is not just a clever intellectual exercise. It is about focussing the mind in deep meditation on Atum (an ancient Egyptian name for God). Such pure philosophy is about rising above mere opinions to experience directly the Mind of the Universe. Using the God-given gift of our own little minds, we can come to know the Big Mind that creates and maintains the Cosmos in beautiful order.

For Hermes, spiritual philosophy is not opposed to science, as it often is for us today. The student of spiritual philosophy studies science as a form of devotion to God. Through understanding the secrets of the natural world, he is overcome with a sense of awe and reverence for the Creator. He appreciates the perfect order of the universe, as if he were listening to a grand symphony in which every melody has been exquisitely combined to compose one magnificent harmony.

Hermes prophesies, however, that this spiritual philosophy will one day become lost and confused. Speaking from our distant past, he uncannily describes the predicament we find ourselves in today. Pure philosophy has been replaced by the teachings of clever intellectuals with no mystical understanding of life. People have ceased to see the universe as a source of wonder, and no longer revere it as the work of God. Spirituality has come to be dismissed by science as primitive superstition. The profound wisdom of the ancient Egyptians is thought of as a dead religion and as little more than an archaeological curiosity. Hermes foretells that Egypt, once the home of spirituality, will become a desolate place deserted by the gods.

Out of compassion for future generations, Hermes writes his wisdom in books and orders them to be hidden. Like a time capsule of truth, Hermes' vision waits for its chance to awaken future generations who are lost and bewildered by life. People such as ourselves.

The Prophecies
of Hermes

Pure philosophy is spiritual striving,
through constant contemplation,
to attain True Knowledge
of Atum the One-God.
But, speaking now in prophecy,
I say that in times to come,
no one will pursue philosophy
with single-mindedness
and purity of heart.
Those with a grudging
and ungenerous temperament
will try and prevent men discovering
the priceless gift of immortality.
Philosophy will become confused,
making it hard to comprehend.
It will be corrupted
by spurious speculation.
It will be entangled with
bewildering sciences
like arithmetic, music and geometry.

The student of pure philosophy
studies the sciences,
not as fanciful theories,
but as devotion to Atum –
because they reveal a universe
perfectly ordered by the power of number;

because measuring the depths of the sea
and forces of fire
and magnitudes of physical things
leads to a reverent awe
at the Creator's skill and wisdom;
because the mysteries of music
bear witness to the unsurpassed talent
of the Supreme Artist
who has beautifully harmonised
all things into a single Whole,
suffused with sweet melodies.

To simply love Atum in thought
with singleness of heart,
and to follow the goodness of his will –
this is philosophy,
unsullied by intrusive cravings
for pointless opinions.
But I foresee that, in times to come,
clever intellectuals
will mislead the minds of men,
turning them away from pure philosophy.
It will be taught that
our sacred devotion was ineffectual
and the heart-felt piety
and assiduous service
with which we Egyptians honour Atum
was a waste without reward.

Egypt is an image of the heavens,
and the whole Cosmos dwells here,
in this its sanctuary –
but the gods will desert the earth
and return to heaven,
abandoning this land
that was once the home of spirituality.

Egypt will be forsaken and desolate,
bereft of the presence of the gods.
It will be overrun by foreigners,
who will neglect our sacred ways.
This holy land of temples and shrines
will be filled with corpses and funerals.
The sacred Nile will be swollen with blood,
and her waters will rise,
utterly fouled with gore.

Does this make you weep?
There is worse to follow.
This land,
that was a spiritual teacher
to all humankind,
which loved the gods with such devotion
that they deigned to sojourn
here on earth –
this land will exceed all others in cruelty.
The dead will far outnumber the living,
and the survivors
will be known as Egyptians
by their language alone,
for in their actions
they will be like men of another race.
O Egypt!
Nothing will remain of your religion
but an empty tale,
which even your own children
will not believe.
Nothing will be left
to tell of your wisdom
but old graven stones.

Men will be weary of life,
and will cease seeing the universe
as worthy of reverent wonder.
Spirituality, the greatest of all blessings,
will be threatened with extinction,
and believed a burden to be scorned.
The world will no longer be loved
as an incomparable work of Atum;
a glorious monument
to his Primal Goodness;
an instrument of the Divine Will
to evoke veneration
and praise in the beholder.

Egypt will be widowed.
Every sacred voice will be silenced.
Darkness will be preferred to light.
No eyes will raise to heaven.
The pure will be thought insane
and the impure will be honoured as wise.
The madman will be believed brave,
and the wicked esteemed as good.
Knowledge of the immortal soul
will be laughed at and denied.
No reverent words worthy of heaven
will be heard or believed.

So I, Thrice-Great Hermes,
the first of men
to attain All-Knowledge,
have inscribed the secrets of the gods,
in sacred symbols and holy hieroglyphs,
on these stone tablets,
which I have concealed
for a future world
that may seek our sacred wisdom.

The Prophecies of Hermes

Through all-seeing Mind,
I myself have been the witness
of the invisible things of Heaven,
and through contemplation
come to Knowledge of the Truth.
This knowing I have set down in these
   writings . . .

II. The Initiation
of Hermes

**In this chapter Hermes describes a
mystical vision of the creation of the
Cosmos, upon which all his later
teachings are based.**

Hermes derives his wisdom from a dramatic mystical reve-
lation. While his mind is alert, yet still and empty, he hears
God speaking to him. Hermes asks to be shown the true
nature of reality, and suddenly everything begins to change
before him.

In a mysterious vision he witnesses the creation of the
world. This vision is not meant to be understood intellectu-
ally, but contemplated like images from a dream. However,
we can explore a little of its deep meaning.

Hermes' first experience is of an all-embracing divine
Light, which as he watches casts a shadow like dark restless
water. Later he is told that this Light is the Mind of God,
and the dark waters are the unlimited potential out of
which God will fashion the universe.

This is a mystical vision of the first act of creation,
remarkably similar to the modern scientific theory of the
Big Bang. An explosion of light and energy slowly cools to
become the black womb of space, into which suns and planets and finally ourselves are born.

This birth, like any birth, is accompanied by pain, and
Hermes hears an inarticulate cry of suffering from the tur-
bulent depths. The Light then speaks a Word which calms
the chaotic waters. This Word is like a blueprint that will

organise a structured cosmos out of the chaos. Modern science might call it the fundamental Laws of Nature. This Word is the first idea in the Mind of God, from which everything springs.

Initiated into the secrets of the creation Hermes receives his divine mission from the Supreme Being. Only this Knowledge he is told can save those who live in darkness. Hermes must become a spiritual guide to all Mankind.

The Initiation
of Hermes

My senses were suspended in mystic sleep –
not a weary, full-fed drowsiness,
but an alert and conscious emptiness.
Released from my body,
I flew with my thoughts,
and while I soared, it seemed to me,
a vast and boundless Being called my name:
'Hermes, what are you looking for?'

'Who are you?' I asked.

'I am the Way-Guide, the Supreme Mind,
the thoughts of Atum the One-God.
I am with you – always and everywhere.
I know your desires.
Make your questions conscious,
and they will be answered.'

'Show me the nature of Reality.
Bless me with Knowledge of Atum,'
I begged.

Suddenly everything changed before me.
Reality was opened out in a moment.
I saw the boundless view.
All became dissolved in Light –
united within one joyous Love.

Yet the Light cast a shadow,
grim and terrible,
which, passing downwards,
became like restless water,
chaotically tossing forth spume like smoke.
And I heard an unspeakable lament –
an inarticulate cry of separation.
The Light then uttered a Word,
which calmed the chaotic waters.

My Guide asked:
'Do you understand the secrets of this vision?
I am that Light – the Mind of God,
which exists before
the chaotic dark waters of potentiality.
My calming Word is the Son of God –
the idea of beautiful order;
the harmony of all things with all things.
Primal Mind is parent of the Word,
just as, in your own experience,
your human mind gives birth to speech.
They cannot be divided, one from the other,
for life is the union of Mind and Word.
Now, fix your attention upon the Light,
and become One with it.'

When he had said this,
he looked into me,
I to I,
until, trembling, I saw in thought
limitless power within the Light,
to form an infinite yet ordered world –
and I was amazed.

I saw in the darkness of the deep,
chaotic water without form
permeated with a subtle intelligent breath
of divine power.
Atum's Word fell on the fertile waters
making them pregnant with all forms.
Ordered by the harmony of the Word,
the four elements came into being,
combining to create the brood of living creatures
The fiery element was articulated
as the constellations of the stars,
and the gods of the seven heavenly bodies,
revolving forever in celestial circles.
The Word then leapt up
from the elements of nature
and reunited with Mind the Maker,
leaving mere matter devoid of intelligence.

My Guide said:
'You have perceived the boundless primal idea,
which is before the beginning.
By Atum's will,
the elements of nature were born
as reflections of this primal thought
in the waters of potentiality.
These are the primary things;
the prior things;
the first principles of all in the universe.
Atum's Word is the creative idea –
the supreme limitless power
which nurtures and provides
for all the things
that through it are created.

I have shown you everything –
why do you wait?
Write the wisdom you have understood
in hieroglyphic characters,
carved on stone in the holy sanctuary.
Make yourself a spiritual guide
to those worthy of the gift of Knowledge,
so that, through you,
Atum may save humankind.'

I was overwhelmed with gratitude
to the All-Father who had graced me
with the supreme vision.
In awe and reverence I prayed,
'Please never let me fall away
from this Knowledge of your Being,
so that I may enlighten
those who are in darkness.'

Then, with his power in me,
I began to speak.
The aloof laughed at my words,
but others knelt at my feet.
I told them to stand
and receive the seeds of wisdom,
which I will sow in you
with these teachings.

So, listen, men of clay.
If you do not pay keen attention,
my words will fly past you,
and wing their way back to the source
from which they come.

III. The Being of Atum

In this chapter Hermes attempts to describe God (Atum). Although God cannot be defined with words, Hermes gives some clues for us to contemplate.

God is Oneness. Everything is a part of one Supreme Being. Like the number one, which is the source of all subsequent numbers, God is the source of all. Yet just as when the number one is divided or multiplied by itself it remains one, so God constantly remains the Oneness.

Because he unites every thing, his nature is paradoxical. He is the creator who creates himself. He is always hidden from us, yet he is also the world around us. He has no particular name, because all names refer to him.

God is the Supreme Mind. He is everywhere and always. The human mind is an image of the Supreme Mind. Through the power of the imagination it can roam the universe and be, like God, in all times and all places. Hermes tells us that if we truly understood the extraordinary power of the human mind, we would then know the nature of God.

Everything exists as an idea within the Mind of God. He creates all things, in the same way that our own minds create thoughts. Just as the nature of mind is to think, so the nature of God is to create. This is not something he did at the beginning of time. He is doing it continuously. God is 'constantly creating creation', and will never stop.

God is both the material objects around us and the immaterial thoughts in our minds. The world we see and sense is an illusion, however, compared to the great ideas which only exist in the mind. Above all are the ideas of Goodness and Beauty. These qualities belong to God alone. They can at best be found imperfectly in the material world, but exist in all their perfection in the immaterial world of the mind. They are so perfect that God is in love with them. God is in love with himself.

The Being of Atum

Give me your whole awareness,
and concentrate your thoughts,
for Knowledge of Atum's Being
requires deep insight,
which comes only as a gift of grace.
It is like a plunging torrent of water
whose swiftness outstrips any man
who strives to follow it,
leaving behind not only the hearer,
but even the teacher himself.

To conceive of Atum is difficult.
To define him is impossible.
The imperfect and impermanent
cannot easily apprehend
the eternally perfected.
Atum is whole and constant.
In himself he is motionless,
yet he is self-moving.
He is immaculate,
incorruptible and ever-lasting.
He is the Supreme Absolute Reality.
He is filled with ideas
which are imperceptible to the senses,
and with all-embracing Knowledge.
Atum is Primal Mind.

He is too great
to be called by the name 'Atum'.
He is hidden,
yet obvious everywhere.
His Being is known through thought alone,
yet we see his form before our eyes.
He is bodiless,
yet embodied in everything.
There is nothing which he is not.
He has no name,
because all names are his name.
He is the unity in all things,
so we must know him by all names
and call everything 'Atum'.

He is the root and source of all.
Everything has a source,
except this source itself,
which springs from nothing.
Atum is complete like the number one,
which remains itself
whether multiplied or divided,
and yet generates all numbers.

Atum is the Whole
which contains everything.
He is One, not two.
He is All, not many.
The All is not many separate things,
but the Oneness that subsumes the parts.
The All and the One are identical.
You think that things are many
when you view them as separate,
but when you see they all hang on the One,

and flow from the One,
you will realise they are united –
linked together,
and connected by a chain of Being
from the highest to the lowest,
all subject to the will of Atum.

The Cosmos is one as the sun is one,
the moon is one and the Earth is one.
Do you think there are many Gods?
That's absurd – God is one.
Atum alone is the Creator
of all that is immortal,
and all that is mutable.
If that seems incredible, just consider yourself.
You see, speak, hear, touch,
taste, walk, think and breathe.
It is not a different you
who does these various things,
but one being who does them all.

To understand how Atum makes all things,
consider a farmer sowing seeds;
here wheat – there barley,
now planting a vine – then an apple tree.
Just as the same man plants all these seeds,
so Atum sows immortality in heaven
and change on Earth.
Throughout the Cosmos
he disseminates Life and movement –
the two great elements
that comprise Atum and his creation,
and so everything that is.

Atum is called 'Father'
because he begets all things,
and, from his example,
the wise hold begetting children
the most sacred pursuit of human life.
Atum works with Nature,
within the laws of Necessity,
causing extinction and renewal,
constantly creating creation
to display his wisdom.

Yet, the things that the eye can see
are mere phantoms and illusions.
Only those things invisible to the eye are real.
Above all are the ideas of Beauty and Goodness.
Just as the eye cannot see the Being of Atum,
so it cannot see these great ideas.
They are attributes of Atum alone,
and are inseparable from him.
They are so perfectly without blemish
that Atum himself is in love with them.

There is nothing which Atum lacks,
so nothing that he desires.
There is nothing that Atum can lose,
so nothing can cause him grief.
Atum is everything.
Atum makes everything,
and everything is a part of Atum.
Atum, therefore, makes himself.
This is Atum's glory – he is all-creative,
and this creating is his very Being.
It is impossible for him ever to stop creating –
for Atum can never cease to be.

The Being of Atum

Atum is everywhere.
Mind cannot be enclosed,
because everything exists within Mind.
Nothing is so quick and powerful.
Just look at your own experience.
Imagine yourself in any foreign land,
and quick as your intention
you will be there!
Think of the ocean – and there you are.
You have not moved as things move,
but you have travelled, nevertheless.
Fly up into the heavens –
you won't need wings!
Nothing can obstruct you –
not the burning heat of the sun,
or the swirling planets.
Pass on to the limits of creation.
Do you want to break out
beyond the boundaries of the Cosmos?
For your mind, even that is possible.
Can you sense what power you possess?
If you can do all this,
then what about your Creator?
Try and understand that Atum is Mind.
This is how he contains the Cosmos.
All things are thoughts
which the Creator thinks.

IV. Contemplate Creation

In this chapter Hermes teaches us how to see God by contemplating his creation.

When we look at the world only with our physical eyes, God is nowhere to be seen. But if we look with our thoughts, we see with spiritual understanding. Suddenly God is everywhere. In this ecstatic state everything we see and touch is known to be a part of God, and we understand that God's whole purpose in creating the world was so that through it we could see him.

The Cosmos is his body, and we can come to know him by contemplating its extraordinary order and beauty. Hermes asks us to consider the constant revolutions of the stars in the night sky; the laws of fate, which he calls Necessity; the goodness of everything that has happened and is happening. Could this all be so perfect without a Supreme Mind which maintains such exquisite order? Could it all just be happening accidentally?

He reminds us of the marvel of our own birth. Who created us in the womb? Who perfectly crafted the individual details of our bodies? Statues and portraits don't just happen, they are sculpted and painted. Surely such a work of art as beautiful and complex as our own physical forms must be the work of a master craftsman? The modern view is that we are a creation of the laws of nature. Hermes would not disagree with this; he would simply ask, 'Who decreed these laws?'

He is trying to return us to a childlike sense of awe in the face of the wonders of life. The world is a miracle, yet we take it for granted. If we take the time to reflect, it becomes obvious that we are surrounded by profound mysteries. The universe is a gigantic work of art, signed by an unknown master. Humble amazement is a prerequisite for coming to know God.

Contemplate Creation

Ask Atum
to flash a ray of his illumination
into your awareness,
giving you the power
to grasp in thought
his sublime Being.
For the invisible
may only be seen with thoughts –
which are themselves invisible.

If you can't see thoughts,
do you expect to see Atum?
Look with your mind, however,
and he will appear to you,
manifesting himself without reservation
throughout the whole universe,
so that you may see his image with your eyes
and hold it with your two hands.

Do you think Atum is invisible?
Don't say that!
Nothing is more visible than Atum.
He created all things so that through them
you could see him.
This is Atum's Great Heart –
that he manifests himself in everything.

Everything can be known,
including the insubstantial.
Just as Mind is known through thoughts,
so Atum is known through his creation.

Atum is the all-encompassing author of entirety,
weaving everything into the fabric of reality.
Because creation is visible,
we can see the Creator,
and this is the purpose of his creation.
Since he is always creating,
he can always be seen,
so we should think and marvel,
and realise that we are blessed
with Knowledge of our Father.

To know Atum's Being,
contemplate him in thought.
To see him with your eyes,
look at the exquisite order of the Cosmos;
the Necessity which governs
everything you perceive;
the Goodness of all that has been,
and that is coming to be.
Look at matter filled full with Life,
and see Atum
pulsating with all he contains.

Contemplate the Cosmos
as his ancient body,
which is ever prime and new.
See the planets circling in eternal time.
See the spiritual fire of the heavens
turned to light by the sun
and shed as Goodness upon the world.

See the ever-changing moon,
which governs birth, growth and decay.
See the constellation of the Bear
which never rises or sets,
but stays ever a fixed point –
an axle around which
the circle of the Zodiac revolves.
See the comets
which are called 'Prophet Stars',
for when some future fate awaits the world
they emerge for a few days,
from their invisible home
below the circle of the sun.
Who is it that maintains such exquisite order?

The sun is the greatest god in the heavens –
a king to whom all the others pay homage.
Yet, this mighty god humbly submits
to have smaller stars circle above him.
Who is it that he obeys with awe?
Each star travels its appointed range of space.
Why don't all stars run the same course?
Who is it who has assigned to each its place?
The Bear revolves around herself
and carries around with her the whole Cosmos.
Who is it that appointed her this task?
Who is it that fixed the Earth,
and confined the sea within its shores?
Someone must be the maker and master of all this
It couldn't just happen.
All order must be created.
It is only that which is out of measure
which is accidental.
Yet even disorder is subject to the Master,
who has yet to impose order upon it.

If only it were possible to grow wings
and soar into the air –
poised between heaven and Earth,
you would see the solid ground,
the flowing rivers, the wandering air,
the penetrating fire, the circling stars,
and the encompassing heavens.
What joy to see all this,
borne along by the one impulse –
to perceive the unmoved mover
moving in all that moves.
He who is hidden,
manifest through all his works.

Consider for a moment,
how you were created in the womb.
Think of that skilful workmanship,
and look for the craftsman
who made such a beautiful God-like image.
Who traced the circles of your eyes?
Who pierced your nostrils, ears and mouth?
Who stretched your sinews and tied them fast?
Who built your bones
and wrapped your flesh with skin?
Who separated your fingers
and flattened your feet?
Who shaped your heart
and hollowed your lungs?
Who made your beauty visible,
and concealed your guts within?
How many crafts have been employed,
and how many works of art created
to form one human being?
Statues or portraits don't just happen
without a sculptor or painter.
Has such a sublime work no creator?

V. The Living Cosmos

In this chapter Hermes succinctly outlines the essence of his philosophical ideas, and paints the picture of the Cosmos as a living being, teeming with life.

In the beginning there is unity. Unity separates into two fundamental forces, which like the negative and positive poles of a battery, generate everything. Hermes describes them as Light and Life, which become Mind and Soul. We experience them as thoughts and feelings.

The Oneness of God is both Light and Life. These two forces are the parents of the Mind of the Cosmos. This was experienced by Hermes in his original mystical vision as the 'Word' which calmed the dark waters – the fundamental laws of nature which bring order to the chaos.

The physical Cosmos is a perfect reflection of this ordering principle – the Mind of the Cosmos. The Mind of the Cosmos (the Word) is in turn a reflection of God, just as a spoken word reflects the intention of its speaker. Since God is All-Goodness, the Cosmos is therefore also Good.

Because the Cosmos is made in the image of its Creator it too is an immortal living being. It is therefore impossible that any part of it can be dead. At its conception it was filled with energy, which as modern science has now proved can neither be created or destroyed. Unlike the myriad forms that it passes through, energy itself is immortal.

God is the source of this energy which, through the

laws of Nature, creates life. The Cosmic Mind receives energy from God and gives it to all the things within the Cosmos. Through this process, the Cosmos is completely saturated with Soul – the Life-Force. Everything in it is alive. Nothing is dead, not even so called inanimate things. The Cosmos is a great living being which in turn gives Life to all the lesser beings it contains. It is the whole which nourishes its parts, like a parent caring for its children.

The Living Cosmos

The Primal Mind,
which is Life and Light,
being bisexual,
gave birth to the Mind of the Cosmos.
The Primal Mind is ever unmoving,
eternal and changeless,
containing within it this Cosmic Mind
which is imperceptible to the senses.
The Cosmos which sense perceives
is a copy and image
of this eternal Cosmic Mind,
like a reflection in a mirror.

First of all
and without beginning is Atum.
Second is the Cosmos,
made in his likeness.
As the Cosmos is a second god,
it is also an immortal being,
and because every thing in the Cosmos
is a part of the Cosmos,
it is impossible that any part of it should die.
The Cosmos is all Life.
From its first foundations
there has never existed a single thing
which was not alive.

There is not,
and has never been,
and never will be,
anything in the Cosmos that is dead.

Atum is Light –
the everlasting source of Energy,
the eternal dispenser of Life Itself.
Once Energy has been dispensed,
its supply is governed by eternal cosmic laws.
The Cosmos has its being
within the Eternal Energy
from which all Life issues,
so it is impossible for it ever to stop
or be destroyed.
It is contained and bound together
by the Eternal Life-Force.
The Cosmos dispenses this Life
to all the things within it.
It has a twofold movement –
Energy is infused into the Cosmos from Eternity
and it in turn infuses Life into all things within it.

Mind and Soul
are manifestations of Light and Life.
Everything moves by the power of Soul.
The body of the Cosmos,
within which all bodies are contained,
is completely saturated with Soul.
Soul is entirely illuminated by Mind.
Mind is totally permeated by Atum.
Soul fills and encompasses
the whole body of the Cosmos.

It gives Life
to the great and perfect living creature
which is the Cosmos,
which in turn gives Life
to all the lesser living creatures it contains.
The Cosmos is the whole
which generates and nourishes the parts,
like a parent caring for its children.
It receives its supply of Goodness from Atum,
and it is this Goodness
which is the true power of creation.
The Cosmos is the image of Atum,
and since Atum is All-Goodness,
the Cosmos is also Good.

VI. The Circle of Time

**In this chapter Hermes explores the
nature of time and change.**

Everything in the Cosmos is constantly changing. Things
are born, pass away and come into existence again, like old
plants dying each winter to return as new shoots each
spring. All these changes, however, are governed by
unchanging natural laws. In this way, therefore, it could
also be said that the Cosmos is essentially changeless.

Time regulates the natural processes of change in the
Cosmos. It is measured by the recurring cycles of the stars
and the sun, which revolve in fixed and permanent orbits.
Unlike our modern picture of time as a straight line from
the past to the future, Hermes sees time as a circle. We too
actually measure time in circles, however. A day is a circle
of time which begins again when the sun rises each morn-
ing. The year is a circle of time measured by the Earth's
orbit around the sun. Vaster circles of time are expressed by
the movements of the constellations of the stars. All of these
cycles eventually bring things back to where they started. It
is impossible to say where that is, however, for a circle has
no starting point – you cannot say where it begins and
where it ends.

Hermes ultimately points to a deeper understanding of
time. The past has gone and does not exist. The future has
yet to happen and does not exist. The present moment
passes so quickly that it has no permanence. Before we have
even said 'now', the moment has gone. We can never catch

the present, so in what way could it be said to exist? This mystical insight into the illusory nature of time is a way to glimpse the Oneness of God, who exists beyond time. For God, there is no past, present and future – only eternity. Freeing ourselves from the illusion of time is yet another way we can experience God.

The Circle of Time

In a sense, the Cosmos is changeless,
because its motions are determined
by unalterable laws
which cause it to revolve eternally
without beginning and end.
Its parts manifest, disappear
and are created anew,
again and again
in the undulating pulse of time.

Through the process of time,
life within the Cosmos
is regulated and maintained.
Time renews all things in the Cosmos,
by the circling process of change,
measured by the heavenly bodies
returning to their former positions
as they revolve around the heavens.

The present issues from the past,
and the future from the present.
Everything is made one by this continuity.
Time is like a circle,
where all the points are so linked
that you cannot say
where it begins or ends,
for all points both precede
and follow one another for ever.

Yet, there is an even deeper understanding.
The past has departed and no longer is.
The future has not arrived and is yet to be.
Even the present does not last,
so how can it be said to exist,
when it doesn't stay still for a moment?

VII. The Gods

**In this chapter Hermes discusses
the many powers through which
God administers creation.**

To the ancient Egyptians the night sky was seen as the body of the black goddess sprinkled with stars. In the Hermetica she is known as the great goddess Destiny, whose unalterable laws are written in the unchanging star-fields of the constellations. Against the background of these stars circle the planets, ruled by the great goddess they administer her fate to all things upon the Earth.

Although the constellations of the stars contain the Destiny of everything, the five visible planets and the sun and moon are the forces which administer this Destiny. Hermes therefore calls these powers 'gods'.

Destiny, working through the planetary gods, governs all of creation. They pour an uninterrupted stream of Life-force into all forms of matter, making them ceaselessly change from one state to another in a process we call living and dying. The gods are ruled by the goddess Destiny who makes sure that all they do accords with God's will.

The god Ra is the sun which sends down energy to the Earth. Whilst God is the hidden Light which cannot be seen with the physical eyes because it is pure energy, Ra is the visible light placed at the centre of our solar system.

The sun is an image of God, and as God gives Life to the whole universe, so the sun gives life to the animals and plants of the Earth. The light of the sun nurtures nature in the same way that the Light of God nurtures our souls.

The Gods

The Mind of the Cosmos
created from fire and air
the seven administrators
who regulate Destiny –
the five visible planets
and the sun and moon
whose orbits encompass
the world of the senses.
These celestial powers,
known by thought alone,
are called the gods,
and they preside over the world.
They are ruled over by the goddess Destiny,
who transforms everything
according to the law of natural growth,
creating from the permanent
unchanging Reality,
a permanently changing world.

The heavenly bodies
are governed by Atum,
and from them flows into matter
an uninterrupted stream of Soul.
Matter is like a fertile womb
within which all things are conceived.
All forms shape matter
and Soul-Energy ceaselessly changes them –
one into another.

This process is directed by Atum
who infuses each form with Soul
in proportion to its standing
in the scale of Being.
The Earth is the storehouse of all matter,
which it donates and, in return,
it receives Life from above.

Ra, the sun, unites heaven and Earth,
sending down Energy from above
and raising up matter from below.
He draws Life to himself
and gives forth Life from himself –
ceaselessly lavishing light on all.
Ra benefits not only heaven,
but even the hidden depths of the Earth.
Unlike Atum, the hidden Light,
who is only known in thought
through attentive contemplation,
Ra exists in space and time,
and we may see him with our eyes,
shinning the brightest in the Cosmos.
Placed in the centre
and wearing the Cosmos
like a wreath around him,
he lights up above and below.
He lets the Cosmos go on its way,
but never lets it wander,
for, like a skilful chariot driver,
Ra has tied the Cosmos to him,
preventing it rushing off in disorder –
and his controlling reins are rays of light.

The sun is an image of the Creator
who is higher than the heavens.

Just as that supreme Creator
gave Life to the whole universe,
Ra gives Life
to the animals and plants.
His material body
is the source of visible light,
and, if there be such a thing as a substance
not perceptible to the senses,
the light of the sun
must contain that substance.
Yet what it is or how it flows –
only Atum knows.

The sun continuously pours forth Light and Life.
Ra nurtures all vegetation,
gathering the first fruits
produced by the power of his rays,
as if in his mighty hands,
bringing out sweet perfumes from the plants.
In the same way,
our souls, like heavenly flowers,
are nurtured by the Light of Atum's wisdom,
and in return,
we should use in his service
all that grows within us.

VIII. The Hierarchy of Creation

**In this chapter Hermes
summarises his teachings on
the way in which God creates
and maintains the Cosmos and
all it contains.**

God creates an ordering principle – the Mind of the
Cosmos. This ordering principle continually organises
chaotic matter into a beautifully ordered physical Cosmos.
Time is one of the principles by which the Cosmos is
ordered. The existence of time means that everything
within the Cosmos is constantly changing, but in a measured way.

God is the Goodness that creates Life. The Mind of the
Cosmos is the fundamental laws of nature – the permanent
and unchanging principles which govern Life. The physical
Cosmos is the beautiful order of nature within which Life
exists. Time is the governing principle of the Cosmos which
produces change. Constant change is the process of everything living and dying.

The Cosmic Mind is an idea expressed by the Mind of
God. The physical Cosmos is a thought expressed by the
Mind of the Cosmos. At the heart of the Cosmos is the life-
giving sun which is an image of the life-giving soul at the
heart of every person.

The Hierarchy of Creation

Atum creates the Cosmic Mind.
The Cosmic Mind creates the Cosmos.
The Cosmos creates Time.
Time creates Change.

The essence of Atum
is Primal Goodness.
The essence of the Cosmic Mind
is permanent sameness.
The essence of the Cosmos
is beautiful order.
The essence of Time
is movement.
The essence of Change is Life.

Atum works
through Mind and Soul.
The Cosmic Mind works
through immortality and duration.
The Cosmos works
through turning and returning.
Time works
through increase and decrease.
Change works
through quality and quantity.

The Cosmic Mind is in Atum.
The Cosmos is in Eternity.
Time is in the Cosmos.
Change is in Time.

The Cosmic Mind
is permanently connected to Atum.
The Cosmos is made up of thoughts
in the Cosmic Mind.

The Cosmic Mind is an image of Atum.
The Cosmos is an image of the Cosmic Mind.
The sun is an image of the Cosmos.
Man is an image of the sun.

IX. The Creation
of Humankind

**Having discussed the principles by
which God created the Cosmos, in
this chapter Hermes describes the
making of mankind.**

God created humankind because he wanted there to be a
creature capable of appreciating the great beauty of his
Cosmos. He asks each of the gods who administer the
Cosmos to provide something to benefit humanity. The sun
gives joy. The moon gives sleep. Saturn offers the limits of
necessity and the balancing force of justice. Jupiter gives
peace and Mars gives struggle. Venus offers love and
Mercury wisdom.

When God hears what the gods will offer, he thinks
humankind into existence. At first humanity is just a
thought – a soul. It is unable to tend and look after the
Earth as God wishes, so God gives each human a mortal
body within which to house the immortal soul. To do this
he first creates Nature. She is like a beautiful woman, and
God makes her mistress of the world. She produces the
seeds of natural life. Seeing in the human soul an image of
God, Nature falls in love and merges with her beloved. This
is the blending of body and soul which produces each one
of us. Hence all human beings have a dual nature, being a
combination of an immortal soul and a mortal body. We
honour both sides of our nature when we serve God by
administering the natural world for him.

Finally God gives humankind a last great gift – the

ability to reproduce. More than this, he makes the process a holy loving sacrament which reflects the marriage of matter and spirit that creates the Cosmos. The sacred bond of love unites man and woman together, so that they may share their essential qualities with each other.

The Creation
of Humankind

When the Creator,
who, for want of a better name,
we call 'Atum',
had made the 'second god',
which is the Cosmos,
he was pleased.
His creation was beautiful,
and wholly filled with goodness,
and he loved it like his child.

In his kindness,
Atum wished for there to be a creature
capable of appreciating
the beauty of his creation.
So, by an act of will,
he created humankind,
to be an imitator of his divine wisdom
and nurturing love.

Atum asked each heavenly god in turn,
'What can you provide for humanity,
which I am about to create?'
The sun said it would shine all day,
providing laughter as a source of joy
for both mortal minds
and the boundless universe itself.
The moon promised sleep and silence,
and to shine by night.

Saturn offered justice and necessity.
Jupiter gave peace and Mars struggle.
Venus proffered love and pleasure.
Mercury, who is also called Hermes,
said: 'I will make humankind intelligent.
I will convey to them wisdom
and Knowledge of the Truth.
I will never cease to benefit all humanity.'
Atum was glad when he heard these words
and gave the command
that man should come into being.

Mind, the All-Father,
who is Life and Light,
gave birth to humanity,
which bore his own image,
and he took delight in his offspring.
Joined to the gods by a sense of kinship,
humanity worshipped them
with piety and holy thoughts,
while, for their part,
the gods watch over humankind
with concern and loving mercy.

At first man was solely eternal and spiritual,
but Atum saw that his new creation
could not tend the Earth
unless he sheltered him in a material envelope –
giving man a mortal body
as well as an immortal soul.
So, Atum bade Nature be,
and from his voice came a woman's form,
so lovely that the gods
were smitten with her beauty.
Atum made Nature mistress of the world.

The Creation of Humankind

She communed with herself,
producing all kinds of seeds
which Atum took hold of with his hands
and scattered over the Earth,
who is the mother of all worldly things.
Seeing in man a beautiful image of Atum,
Nature was filled with insatiable love.
She clasped him to her,
and they merged to become one in love.
Mortal and eternal blended and mingled
so that Man may perform the demands
of both sources of his nature.
Firstly, to serve God –
venerating and praising the things of heaven.
Secondly, to assist
and administer the things of Earth,
by tilling the soil, navigating the waters,
building on the land,
and by serving each other –
that strongest of bonds
that links the human race together.

Then Atum,
the master of generation,
bestowed on humankind
the sacrament of reproduction –
full of affection and joy,
gladness and yearning,
and all the heavenly love that is his Being.

I would have to explain the nature
of this compelling sacred bond
that binds a man and woman together,
were it not that each one of us,
if we explore our innermost feelings,
can experience it for ourselves.

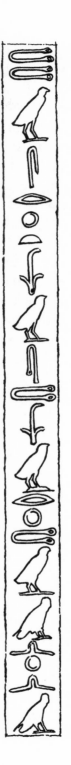

Contemplate that supreme moment,
when each sex infuses itself with the other.
One giving forth
and the other eagerly embracing.
At that moment,
through the intermingling of the two natures,
the female acquires male vigour,
and the male is relaxed in female languor.
This sweet sacramental act we celebrate
is shared in secret,
because if performed openly
before impure eyes,
the ignorant may mock
and the divine power
manifesting in both sexes
will shy away.

X. The Birth of
Human Culture

In this chapter Hermes describes how human beings became civilised and created culture, under the guidance of the god Osiris and goddess Isis.

As human beings slowly awoke to their surroundings, they looked around at their new home and gazed on the creation in awe and wonder. Looking upon the perfection of the Cosmos humanity felt the need to share in the pleasure of creativity. The Creator therefore ordered each of the planetary gods to share with mankind a part of their creative power.

The Hermetica teaches that the universe will not be finished until mankind has played his part in the story. The arts and sciences invented by humanity complete the grand plan of Destiny, art completes what nature cannot finish. All those who cooperate with the will of the Creator apply their skill and knowledge to enhance the beauty of the Cosmos.

The ancient Egyptians believed that all the knowledge necessary for humanities survival on Earth had been taught to their ancestors by Isis and Osiris. The goddess Isis taught people the arts of sowing and animal husbandry ensuring that they did not starve, and she showed them the healing uses of herbs and medicine to care for the body. She taught people respect for the dead, how to wrap their bodies in bandages soaked in oil and spices and to care for their memories with offerings of fruits and flowers. Osiris gave people laws and justice, and instituted the rites of worship that kept men humble and honest. He ordained the first priests who were trained to nurture men's souls through the proper use of philosophy and learning.

Together these parents of the human race were believed by the ancient Egyptians to have lifted their ancestors out of savagery. In life Isis continued to look after humanity, and Osiris the 'Lord of Souls' watched over the spirits of the dead. They were worshipped for thousands of years at temples all over Egypt until late Roman times.

The Birth of
Human Culture

Humanity looked in awe
upon the beauty
and everlasting duration of creation.
The exquisite sky flooded with sunlight.
The majesty of the dark night,
lit by celestial torches
as the holy planetary powers
trace their paths in the heavens
in fixed and steady metre –
ordering the growth of things
with their secret infusions.
Men looked with wonder and questioning,
and, having observed the Maker's masterpiece,
wanted to create things for themselves.
Their Father gave permission,
so the gods who administer the Cosmos
each shared with humanity a part of their power

Since the world is Atum's handiwork,
those who maintain and enhance its beauty
are co-operating with the will of Atum
by contributing their bodily strength
in daily care and labour
to make things assume the shape
which his purpose has designed.
Chance is movement without order,
and skill is the force which creates order.

The Earth is kept in order
by means of humanity's knowledge
and application of the arts and sciences –
for Atum willed that the universe
should not be complete
until man had played his part.

Atum, the fabricator of the Cosmos,
graced the Earth for a little time
with our great father Osiris
and the great goddess Isis,
that they might give us
the help we so much needed.
They brought humanity divine religion
and stopped the savagery
of mutual slaughter.
They established rites of worship,
in correspondence to the sacred powers
of the heavens.
They consecrated temples,
and instituted sacrificial offerings to the gods
that were their ancestors.
They gave the gifts of food and shelter.
They taught men to swathe
the decaying corpses of the dead.
Having learnt Atum's secret laws,
they became lawgivers to humankind.
They introduced the mighty god of oaths
as founder of pledges and good faith,
and so filled the world with justice.
They devised the initiation and training
of the prophet-priests,
so that through philosophy
they might nurture men's souls,
and cure sickness of the body
with the healing arts.

XI. Man Is a Marvel

In this chapter Hermes discusses the nature of mankind and its special relationship with God.

God, the Cosmos and man are the three great beings. The Cosmos is an image of God, and man is an image of the Cosmos. Each is made up of many parts, yet each is greater than the sum of these parts. Man was created to be a vehicle through which God could continue to bring order and beauty to the Cosmos. All beings have Soul – the Life-Force – within them. But only human beings possess the power of Mind, with which we can contemplate the Cosmos and come to know God.

Human beings are the meeting place of spirit and matter. We have, therefore, a dual nature. We are Mind enclosed by a physical body. The human mind is an image of God's Mind – it is immortal, eternal, divine and free. The human body, on the other hand, is mortal and controlled by the laws of Destiny which are governed by the stars.

Hermes dares to suggest that this unique dual nature even places human beings above the gods. The gods – the heavenly bodies – are confined within their permanent orbits in the heavens, and will never move beyond them. A human being, however, may both be on the Earth and, through the power of his mind, ascend to the heavens. In the twentieth century we have used this power to journey literally to the stars and reach back through telescopes to see the origin of the universe.

Being both spirit and matter, man is an intermediary between these two great principles. He is greater than beings who are merely mortal, and above those who are purely immortal. He shares in the creative power of God. He even, with his mind, creates gods in his own human image.

Hermes concludes that man is a marvel, worthy of wonder and reverence – a sentiment that fuelled the humanism of the Renaissance. The purpose of human life is to rise above our merely human nature and awaken our divine nature. Human beings have the unique potential to know God, and God's greatest wish is that we fulfil this potential.

Man Is a Marvel

Atum is first,
the Cosmos is second,
and man is third.
Atum is One,
the Cosmos is One,
and so is man –
for like the Cosmos
he is a whole made up
of different diverse parts.
The Maker made man
to govern with him,
and if man accepts this function fully,
he becomes a vehicle
of order in the Cosmos.

Man may know himself,
and so know the Cosmos,
by being aware
that he is an image of Atum
and of the Cosmos.
He differs from other living things
in that he possesses Mind.
Through Mind he may commune
with the Cosmos, which is the second god –
and by thought he may come to Knowledge
of Atum the One-God.

The human body encloses pure Mind,
as if within a walled garden,
which shelters and secludes it,
so that it may live in peace.
Man has this two-fold nature –
in his body he is mortal,
and in his intelligence he is immortal.
He is exalted above heaven,
but is born a slave to Destiny.
He is bisexual,
as his Father is bisexual.
He is sleepless,
as his Father is sleepless.
Yet he is dominated by carnal desires,
and lost in forgetfulness.
Of all beings that have Soul,
only man has a two-fold nature.
One part, called 'The Image of Atum',
is single, undivided, spiritual and eternal.
The other part
is made of the four material elements.
One comes from the Primal Mind.
It has the power of the Creator,
and is able to know Atum.
The other is put in man
by the revolution of the heavens.

Man is the most divine of all beings,
for amongst all living things,
Atum associates with him only –
speaking to him in dreams at night,
foretelling the future for him
in the flight of birds,
the bowels of beasts
and the whispering oak.

All other living things
inhabit only one part of the Cosmos –
fishes in water,
animals on the earth,
birds in the air.
Man penetrates all of these elements.
With his sense of sight,
he even grasps the heavens.

To speak without fear,
human beings are above the gods of heaven,
or at least their equal –
for the gods will never pass
their celestial boundaries
and descend to Earth,
but a man may ascend to heaven,
and what is more,
he may do so without leaving the Earth,
so vast an expanse
can his power encompass.
By Atum's will,
humankind is compacted,
of both divinity and mortality.
He is more than merely mortal,
and greater than the purely immortal.

Man is a marvel,
due honour and reverence.
He takes on the attributes of the gods,
as if he were one of their number.
He is familiar with the gods,
because he knows he springs
from the same source.
He raises reverent eyes to heaven above,
and tends the Earth below.
He is blessed by being the intermediary.

He loves all below him,
and is loved by all above him.
Confident of his divinity,
he throws off his solely human nature.
He has access to all.
His keenness of thought
descends to the depths of the sea.
Heaven is not too high
for the reach of his wisdom.
His quick wits penetrate the elements.
Air cannot blind his mental vision
with its thickest fog.
Dense earth cannot impede him.
Deep water cannot blur his gaze.
Man is all things.
Man is everywhere.

Man not only receives the Light of divine Life,
but gives it as well.
He not only ascends to God,
but even creates gods.
Just as Atum has willed
that the inner man
be created in his likeness,
so we on Earth create the gods
in our human image.
Is this not worthy of wonder?

There are then these three –
Atum, Cosmos, man.
The Cosmos is contained by Atum.
Man is contained by the Cosmos.
The Cosmos is the son of Atum.
Man is the son of the Cosmos,
and the grandson, so to speak, of Atum.

Man Is a Marvel

Atum does not ignore man,
but acknowledges him fully,
as he wishes to be fully acknowledged by man,
for this alone is man's purpose and salvation –
the ascent to heaven
and the Knowledge of Atum.

XII. The Zodiac and Destiny

In this chapter Hermes explains the power of the Zodiac that controls the fate of men, and the possibility of becoming free from its limiting constraints.

God created humans to appreciate the awesome wonder of his universe; to be themselves a beautiful embellishment of the Cosmos; and to share in God's creative powers and participate in the work of creation.

The heavenly gods the planets, who had already bestowed on man some of their own power, now urged the Creator to be cautious. They fear that man will use his inquisitive mind for destructive as well as constructive purposes. Man's powers, they complain, are too great and unlimited, and therefore dangerous to himself and the order of the Cosmos.

God responds to their concerns by creating the Zodiac. This celestial mechanism will control the fate of men and be ruled over by the goddess Destiny. She sows the seeds of a person's fate, which grow and develop under the constraints of Necessity, the limits and demands of physical nature, to shape every human life.

It is a man's lot to live the life prescribed for him by his fate. Very few human beings are capable of escaping from the determining influence of the Zodiac. Man's earthly life is controlled by the power of Destiny, through the physical limitations of the mortal human body. However, if a man's mind is illuminated by the Light of God, he becomes free from these celestial influences – for even the gods are powerless before God. Hermes teaches that it is our duty not simply to acquiesce in our fate, but rather, through intense contemplation of God, to rise above our merely mortal nature and awaken our immortal soul.

The Zodiac
and Destiny

When the Creator
had created this beautifully ordered universe,
he wanted to order the world also.
So, he sent down man –
a mortal creature
made in the image of an immortal being –
to be an embellishment
of the divine body of the Cosmos.
It is man's function
to complete the work of Atum.
He was made to view the universe
with awe and wonder,
and to come to know its Maker.

At first, the heavenly gods complained saying:
'You are being rash in creating humanity.
They see with inquisitive eyes,
and hear what they have no right to hear.
They reach out with audacious hands.
They will dig up the roots of plants,
and investigate the properties of stones.
They will dissect the lower animals –
and one another also!
They will seek to discover
how it is that they are alive,
and what is hidden within.
They will cut down the woods of their native land
and sail across the sea to see what lies there.

They will dig mines
and search the uttermost depths of the Earth.
All this might be bearable,
but they will do much more.
They will press on to explore the world above,
seeking by observation to discover the laws
that govern the movements of the heavens.'

Atum replied:
'I will build the Zodiac –
a secret mechanism in the stars,
linked to unerring and inevitable fate.
The lives of men,
from birth to final destruction,
shall be controlled
by the hidden workings of this mechanism.'

And when the mechanism began to work,
the keen-eyed goddess Destiny
supervised and checked its movements.
Through this mechanism,
Destiny and Necessity are cemented together.
Destiny sows the seed.
Necessity compels the results.
In the wake of Destiny and Necessity
comes order –
the interweaving of events in time.

Atum implants each human soul in flesh
by means of the gods who circle in heaven.
It is man's lot to live his life
according to the fate
determined for him
by these circling celestial powers –
and then to pass away
and be resolved into the elements.

There are some whose name will live on,
through the memorials
of their mighty handiwork,
but the names of the many
will fade into darkness.

Few can escape their fate
or guard against
the terrible influence of the Zodiac –
for the stars are instruments of Destiny,
which bring all things to pass
in the world of men.
If, however,
the rational part of a man's soul
is illuminated by a single ray of Atum's Light,
the workings of these gods is as nothing –
for all gods are powerless
before the Supreme Light.
But such men are few.
Most are led and driven by the gods
which govern earthly life,
using our bodies
as the instruments of Destiny.
To my way of thinking, however,
it is our duty not simply to acquiesce
in our human state,
but, through intense contemplation
of divine things,
to detach ourselves
from our merely mortal nature.

XIII. The Universal and the Particular

In this chapter Hermes clarifies how the Zodiac makes each individual member of the human species unique.

Everything has a 'form'. A table, for example, is a horizontal surface supported by legs. This is the 'universal form' which all tables share. Every individual table shares the universal form of all tables, but it also has a unique particular form by which we know it to be this table and not that one. One table is large and made of oak. Another table is small and made of plastic. Both are unique and yet both are still tables. If anything deviates too far from this universal form we would no longer call it a table. If a table were to be smashed into pieces, for example, it would have changed form and we would now call it something else, 'firewood' perhaps.

Everything is a particular version of a universal form. Every animal for example, is both unique and a member of a particular species. All human beings share the quality of being human, but each individual has unique characteristics by which we may tell them apart from other members of our species. Each one of us is a particular version of the universal form 'human being'.

This quality of humanness is unchanging and permanent. We are very different from our ancestors, but we are no more 'human'. The particular forms are always changing. In a single human life we change from being a baby to become an adult and finally an elder. We never remain the same, yet birth, mortality and death are all contained within the universal form of a human life.

Hermes compares the constant universal forms to the fixed constellations of the stars. He compares the changing particular forms to the changing relationships between the stars as they revolve in the heavens.

Our fundamental human nature remains the same throughout our life, but our individual fate changes in accordance with the constantly changing pattern of the stars. As in astrology, Hermes teaches that our individual destiny is created by the positions of the planets at our moment of birth. These are the 'gods' who take charge of us, controlling our bodies and shaping our souls.

The Universal and the Particular

Atum arranged the constellations of the Zodiac
in harmony with the movements of Nature,
and charged them with producing
all the forms of the animals.
When these gods
had used their different powers,
there emerged four-footed beasts,
creeping things,
fishes and winged birds,
grass and flowering herbs –
all according to their different natures,
and each containing the seed
of the continuance of their species.

Every living thing has its own unique form,
given to it by the power of the Zodiac.
This form is appropriate to its species,
yet each is individual.
The human race, for example,
shares a common universal form
by which we know that a man is a man.
Yet all human beings
have a distinctly different particular form,
of which no two are entirely alike.

Each particular form is unique
because it inhabits
a unique time and place.
The particular forms change
in every moment of every hour,
as the gods of the Zodiac
revolve in their celestial circle.
The universal forms do not change,
just as the constellations remain the same.
But instant by instant,
the particular forms transform,
as the sphere of heaven
changes as it turns.

The sky is wet then dry,
cold then hot,
bright then dark.
But these rapidly alternating forms
are all subsumed
under the universal unchanging form
of the sky.
The Earth is ever-changing,
generating, producing,
yielding different crops –
yet it remains the Earth.
Water may be standing or flowing –
but it is still water.

The human body is an earthly temple
constructed by the power of the Zodiac,
which makes myriad forms
from simple archetypes.
There are twelve signs of the Zodiac
and the forms they produce
fall into twelve divisions.

They are, however,
inseparably united in their action.
Nature makes the human body
so that its constitution resonates
with the patterns of the stars,
in such a way
that they mutually affect one another.

When we are born,
the planetary gods
who are at that time
on duty as ministers of birth
take charge of us.
These particular powers,
that change
according to the rotation of the planets,
make their way in through the body,
and mould the shape of our souls.
They penetrate our nerves and marrow,
veins and arteries,
even our innermost organs.

XIV. Incarnation of the Soul

In this chapter Hermes reveals how souls incarnate into physical bodies.

All souls share the same essential nature. They are neither male nor female, as such differentiating characteristics exist only in the body. All souls are a part of the one Soul of the Cosmos.

God has two servants which look after souls. The Keeper of Souls cares for disembodied souls, and the Conductor of Souls sends them down into physical incarnation. Nature creates the individual body into which a soul incarnates. The power that Hermes calls 'Memory' ensures that this body conforms to the universal 'form' of the human species. The power Hermes calls 'Skill' makes sure that each individual body is a fitting home for the particular soul it houses.

Our individual characteristics are governed by the qualities of the gods presiding over the moment of our incarnation. If the gods present at our birth are peaceful, we will be peaceful by nature. If they are warlike, we will be aggressive. This is why astrologers say, for example, that those born at the time of Aries have certain characteristics whilst those born at the time of Capricorn have a different nature. Those gods who accompany the soul at the moment of birth affect the instinctual nature of the soul. Those that have their effect later in adolescence affect the rational part of the soul.

Before it incarnates, the soul is already wrapped in a spiritual body. When this wrapping is thin and clear, the soul is intelligent. However, when this wrapping is dense and opaque, the soul has limited vision and is only aware of its immediate situation. As a soul sinks into incarnation it forgets its own nature and takes on the qualities of the gods who have shut it into a human body. Hermes describes a vision of disembodied souls about to make their journey into a physical form. They are filled with fear and horror at the fate which awaits them. They cannot bear the prospect of such imprisonment.

Incarnation of the Soul

All souls are parts of one Soul,
which is the Soul of the Cosmos.
Souls all have one nature.
They are neither male nor female.
Such differences of sex
arise only in the body.

In the world above,
there are two gods
who are servants of Atum's Goodness,
called 'The Keeper of Souls'
and 'The Conductor of Souls'.
The Keeper is in charge of disembodied souls.
The Conductor sends down these souls
from time to time, into physical incarnation.
Nature works alongside these gods,
making mortal vessels
into which souls are poured.
Nature also has two assistants
called Memory and Skill.
Memory ensures that Nature
creates individual forms
that are copies of the primal universal forms.

Skill ensures that the individual frame
is fashioned in conformity
with the soul which will embody it –
seeing to it that lively souls have lively bodies,
sluggish souls have sluggish bodies,
powerful souls have powerful bodies.

The soul, which is spiritual,
has its own wrappings,
which are also spiritual.
These are coats made of air.
When such coats are thin and transparent,
the soul is intelligent.
When they are dense and muddied,
like the air in stormy weather,
the soul cannot see far,
but is only aware of its immediate predicament.

The differences in character of the pharaohs
are not determined by the nature of their soul,
for all kingly souls are godlike,
but by the gods
that escort the soul into incarnation.
Souls of such quality,
that incarnate for so high a purpose,
do not descend without attendants –
for divine justice
knows how to assign to each his due,
even when exiled from the Happy Land.
When the soul is accompanied by warlike gods,
this pharaoh will wage war.
When the gods are peaceful,
he will maintain peace.
When they are musical,
he will make music.

When they are just,
he will rule wisely.
When they are lovers of Truth,
he will be a philosopher.
For souls, by necessity,
cling to the temperament of the gods
who bring them down to Earth,
for when they sink into the human condition
they forget their own nature,
and are conscious
only of the disposition of those
who have shut them in this mortal tomb.

The forces which accompany the soul
do not arrive together.
Some enter with the soul
at the moment of birth
and act on the irrational parts of the soul.
The purer forces arrive at adolescence
and co-operate
with the rational part of the soul.

I have seen a vision of souls
about to be shut up in bodies.
Some of them wailed and moaned.
Some struggled against their doom,
like noble beasts caught by crafty hunters
and dragged away from their wild home.
One shrieked
and looking up and down exclaimed:
'O Heaven, source of Being,
bright shining stars
and unfailing sun and moon,

Light and Life-breath of the One,
all you that share our home –
how cruel it is that we are being torn away
from such celestial splendour!
We are to be expelled
from this holy atmosphere
and from the blissful life we live here,
to be imprisoned
in a mean and sorry place.
What hard necessities wait for us?
What hateful thing will we have to do
to meet the needs of a body
that will quickly perish?
Our eyes will see little,
and only through the fluid
which these orbs contain.
And when we see our vast heavenly home
contracted to a size as small as an eye,
our sorrow will never cease.
We shall not even see clearly,
for we have been condemned to darkness.
And when we hear our brothers and sisters
blowing with the wind
we shall grieve
that we are no longer breathing
in unison with them.'

XV. Death and Immortality

In this chapter Hermes explores the nature of death and the fate of the soul which survives it.

From mankind's perspective, time is a destroyer. Through the process of time we age and die. From a cosmic perspective, time is an endlessly repeating cycle, measured by the constant revolutions of the stars. Whilst the things of the Earth are always changing, the orbits of the stars always remain the same. Hermes asks, could something as impermanent and transitory as our earthly existence be regarded as anything other than an illusion? Yet this illusion arises from an underlying permanent reality. The discovery of the permanent within the impermanent is the reward of the spiritual quest.

Hermes teaches that we must accept the inevitable transitory nature of all physical things. Everything is in a process of being born and then dying. The old must pass away so that the new can come into existence. New shoots are born from the decaying remains of old vegetation. And these new shoots will in turn eventually decay and die. He teaches, however, that a human birth is not the beginning of the soul, only of its incarnation as that particular person. Death is simply the end of this particular person and the soul's transformation into another state. Death is just the discarding of a worn-out body. Most people are ignorant of this fact and therefore needlessly fear death.

After leaving the body at death, the individual soul is

judged by the chief of the gods, to see if it is pure and honourable. Pure souls are assigned to a heavenly realm. Ignorant souls fall once again into the material realms and are reincarnated. A soul which during its earthly life has come to know God, will have become all Mind. When it leaves the body it takes on a body of Light and is freed from all limitations. Such an enlightened soul has recognised that its essential nature is god-like, and on death it communes with God. It has 'run the race of purity' and is now completely spiritual and divine. Such a soul has become a 'god'.

Death and Immortality

The end of becoming
is the beginning of destruction.
The end of destruction
is the beginning of becoming.
Everything on Earth must be destroyed,
for without destruction
nothing can be created.
The new comes out of the old.
Every birth of living flesh,
like every growth of crop from seed,
will be followed by destruction.
But from decay comes renewal,
through the circling course
of the celestial gods,
and the power of Nature,
who has her being
in the Being of Atum.

For man, time is a destroyer,
but for the Cosmos
it is an ever-turning wheel.
These earthly forms
that come and go
are illusions.
How can something be real
which never stays the same?
But these transitory illusory things arise
from the underlying permanent reality.

Birth is not the beginning of life –
only of an individual awareness.
Change into another state is not death –
only the ending of this awareness.
Most people are ignorant of the truth,
and therefore afraid of death,
believing it to be the greatest of all evils.
But death is only the dissolution
of a worn-out body.
Our term of service as guardians of the world
is ended when we are freed
from the bonds of this mortal frame
and restored,
cleansed and purified,
to the primal condition of our higher nature.

After quitting the body,
Mind, which is divine by nature,
is freed from all containment.
Taking on a body of Light,
it ranges through all space –
leaving the soul
to be judged and punished,
according to its deserts.
Souls do not all go to the same place.
Nor to different places at random.
Rather, each is allocated
to a place that fits its nature.

When a soul leaves the body
it undergoes a trial and investigation
by the chief of the gods.
When he finds a soul
to be honourable and pure,
he allows it to live in a region
that corresponds to its characteristics.

But if he finds it stained
with incurable ignorance,
he hurls it down
to the storms and whirlwinds,
where it is eternally tossed
between sky and earth
on the billowing air.

Only a good soul is spiritual and divine.
Having wronged no one
and come to know Atum,
such a soul has run the race of purity,
and becomes all Mind.
After it leaves its physical form,
it becomes a spirit in a body of Light,
so that it may serve Atum.

At the dissolution of the body,
first the physical form is transformed
and is no longer visible.
The vital spirit returns to the atmosphere.
The bodily senses go back to the universe,
and recombine in new ways
to do other work.
Then the soul mounts upwards
through the structures of the heavens.
In the first zone,
it is relieved of growth and decay.
In the second,
evil and cunning.
In the third,
lust and deceiving desire.
In the fourth,
domineering arrogance.
In the fifth,
unbalanced audacity and rashness.

In the sixth,
greed for wealth.
In the seventh,
deceit and falsehood.

Having been stripped
of all that was put upon it
by the structures of the heavens,
the soul now possesses
its own proper power
and may ascend
to the eighth sphere –
rejoicing with all those that welcome it,
and singing psalms to the Father.
The gods that dwell above the eighth sphere
sing praises with a voice that is theirs alone,
call each soul to surrender to the gods,
and so each one becomes itself a god
by entering communion with Atum.
This is Primal Goodness.
This is the consummation
of True Knowledge.
Having been initiated into immortality,
a human soul,
now transformed into a god,
joins the gods who dance and sing
in celebration
of the glorious victory of the soul.

XVI. Ignorance of the Soul

In this chapter Hermes explains that human life is an opportunity to come to know God, but that to fulfil this divine purpose we must cease to be enslaved by the body.

The limitations imposed on the soul by the physical body mean that human life is inevitably difficult. But our hope of eternal life rests on how we live our present lives. Earthly existence is an opportunity to train the soul so that, at death, it does not lose its way but travels straight to heaven.

Everything material, even our own body, is foreign to our essential spiritual nature. Unfortunately, we become so caught up with the transitory sensual pleasures of life that we are unaware of our eternal soul. The body should be the slave of the soul, not its master.

Hermes assures us that there is a way to free ourselves from the torments of life. These he tells us are simply caused by our own ignorance. He exhorts us to free ourselves from our enslavement, develop our inner vision, and use the power of our mind to experience the Mind of God. 'Why give yourselves to death when you could be immortal?' he asks.

Hermes assures us that the haven of peace awaits those who rise to his challenge. Man is made in the image of God and can therefore rise to become one with God. Only like can know like. It is our fear that separates us from the truth, our lack of belief in ourselves that binds us to the Earth. Man has the power to ascend into heaven and yet crawls on his belly through the dust. In Hermes' eyes Mankind's greatest error is that he has the power to know God and yet does not use it.

Simply wishing to know God is enough to set us on the road to enlightenment. The spiritual path is not difficult, for as we awaken from our ignorance, God comes to us. At times and places where we least expect it, suddenly we are aware that God is with us. The end of the spiritual journey is the realisation that he is everywhere and everything.

Ignorance of the Soul

It is impossible to be permanently happy
while attached to a body.
A man should train his soul in this life
so that, when he enters the other world
where he is able to see Atum,
he does not lose his way.

Each soul's hope of eternal life
rests in his life here on Earth.
But many cannot believe this,
seeing it as an empty story
to be laughed at –
for the possessions of this life
are too pleasant,
and such pleasures
grip the soul by the throat,
holding it down to Earth.
Our possessions possess us.
We were not born with possessions,
but acquired them later.
Everything a man uses to gratify his body
is alien to his original god-like nature.
Not only possessions –
even the body is foreign
to our true Self.

The Mind of the Cosmos
is known through thought alone.
A soul with no inner vision
is blind to Atum's Goodness –
tossed by the sea of passions
which the body breeds.
What fire burns like impurity?
What hungry predator
has the power to maim the body
as impurity does to mutilate the soul?
Can't you see the torture
that the impure soul endures?
It shrieks:
'I am burning. I am on fire.
I don't know what to say or do.
I am devoured
by the miseries that possess me.'
Are not such cries
the appeals of a soul in torment?
Such a soul bears the body like a burden,
as its master, not as its slave.

Tear off this cloak of shadows.
This web of ignorance.
These shackles of decay.
This living death.
This conscious corpse.
This portable tomb.
This robber in the house.
This enemy that hates all that you love.
This garment that smothers you,
and holds you down.

Ignorance floods the land.
Its currents sweep you away.
Don't be borne downstream.
Make use of the backflow.
Seek the safe haven of liberation.
Anchor there and find a guide
to lead you to the House of Knowledge.
There you will see with the heart,
the brilliant brightness.

If you shut your soul up in your body
and demean yourself, saying,
'I cannot know. I am afraid.
I cannot ascend to heaven.'
Then what have you to do with Atum?
Wake up your sleeping soul.
Why give yourselves to death,
when you could be immortal?
You are drunk with ignorance of Atum.
It has overpowered you,
and now you are vomiting it up.
Empty yourselves of darkness
and you will be filled with Light.

There is no greater mistake
than to have the power to know Atum
and not to use it.
Simply wishing and hoping to know him
is a road that leads straight to Goodness.
It is an easy road to travel.

Everywhere Atum will come to meet you.
Look and he appears –
at times and places when you least expect.
While you are awake or asleep.
When you travel by water or land.
By night or by day.
Whilst you are speaking or silent.
This is because
Atum is All.

XVII. Knowledge of Atum

In this chapter Hermes teaches us how to attain knowledge of God. This, he declares, is the very purpose of human life.

Only like can truly know like, so to know God we must become like God. To do this, Hermes advises us to imagine ourselves in all places at all times; to embrace all opposites; to know we are immortal; to see ourselves as still in the womb and yet already dead. By expanding our consciousness in this way, we can merge with the Mind of God.

Mind is the immortal part of a human being. It is the divine Light which emanates from God. Of all living things, human beings alone have this divine quality, which gives them the potential to know God. Such knowledge is not intellectual opinion. Opinion is only a dim reflection of knowledge. Knowledge is a direct experience of the Truth. It is certain and immediate. An enlightened being does not have opinions about God, he is One with God.

The experience of Mind is like a prize that may be won by human souls. God wants us to immerse ourselves in Mind and so become wholly divine. Yet, those that do are thought mad by the mass of ignorant people. They are laughed at, despised and even put to death. As history shows, this has often been the fate of the wisest saints and sages, such as Socrates and Jesus.

Knowledge of
Atum

To know Atum you must share his identity –
for only like can truly know like.
Leave behind the material world,
and imagine yourself
immeasurably expansive.
Rise out of time to eternity.
Believe that for you
nothing is impossible.
See that you are immortal
and learned in every art and science.
Be at home in the haunts
of every living creature.
Make yourself higher than the highest
and deeper than the depths.
Embrace within yourself all opposites –
heat and cold, hard and fluid.
Think yourself everywhere at once –
on land, at sea, in heaven.
Imagine yourself unborn in the womb,
yet also young and old,
and already dead,
and in the world beyond the grave.
See that everything co-exists within Mind.
All times and all places.
All things of all shapes and sizes.
Then you will know Atum.

If it is possible
to talk of the substance of Atum,
then Mind is the very divine substance –
although only Atum knows its precise nature.
Mind is not separate from Atum,
but emanates from him
like light from the sun.
In human beings,
Mind produces divinity.
Through Mind some become god-like,
for as Osiris teaches:
'Gods are immortal men
and men are mortal gods.'

Mind is the divine part of a human being,
which is capable of rising to heaven.
The material part,
consisting of fire, water, earth and air,
is mortal and remains earthbound
so that he does not abandon the body
that has been entrusted to him.
Soul is nourished by fire and air,
and the body by water and earth.
Mind is the fifth part,
which comes from Light,
and is bestowed on humankind alone.
Of all the beings that have Soul
only human beings,
elevated by this gift of Mind,
may attain Knowledge of Atum.
Such Knowledge is not opinion,
which is only a poor copy of Knowledge –
an echo in comparison with a voice;
the dim reflected light of the moon
compared to the brilliance of the sun.

Mind and speech are great gifts
that Atum bestowed on humans alone.
Used wisely,
they make a man like the immortal gods –
only different
in that he is incarnate in a physical form.
When he leaves behind this body,
Mind and speech will be his guides,
leading him to join the company of gods
and other souls
that have attained the Supreme Bliss.

Other creatures have voice,
but not speech.
Each living creature
has its own unique voice,
but speech is shared
in common by all humans.
Humankind is one
and speech is also one.
It is translated from tongue to tongue.
Yet whether in Egyptian,
Persian or Greek,
the meaning remains the same.
This is because speech
is an image of Mind,
and Mind is an image of Atum.

By Atum's will,
Mind is like a prize
that human souls may win.
He filled a great bowl with Mind
and sent it down to Earth,
telling a herald to announce:
'Listen, every human heart!

Immerse yourself in Mind
and recognise the purpose of your birth.
Ascend to him who sent this bowl.'
Those that bathe themselves in Mind
find True Knowledge
and become complete.
Yet, they are not pleasing
to the mass of men.
They are thought mad and laughed at.
They are hated and despised,
and may even be put to death.

XVIII. Rebirth

**In this chapter Hermes
reveals the secrets of
spiritual rebirth, through
which we can awaken to
our immortal soul.**

The inexorable working of destiny, imposed on man by the turning of the Zodiac, subjects all human beings to the pain of birth and death. Man's problem is that in his ignorance he believes himself to be just a body, one that will grow old, suffer and eventually die. His sense of injustice at the inevitability of this fate leads him to hurt himself and others, either through lust for more life or fear of approaching death. These crimes serve further to bind the soul to the body and so increase man's suffering. Purifying ourselves of ignorance is therefore the first step on the ladder that leads to rebirth. Rebirth is the Knowledge of our own immortality.

To escape the suffering inherent in our human predicament, we must be reborn in spirit. The spiritual path that we must walk is the same one trodden by our ancestors. It is a hard road to follow whilst incarnate in a physical body, because we must struggle to master ourselves. Right understanding purifies us of all the vices that torment us and awakens our immortal soul.

One who is thus reborn communes with God. But this only happens when we stop talking about it and allow it to occur naturally in the silence and tranquillity of deep contemplation. An enlightened being no longer believes he is a body. The body belongs to Nature, not to him, and so its fate is of no importance. He is One with everything. He sees Goodness everywhere. He is ba⁺hed in divine Light. He has become All-Mind.

Rebirth is not a theory that we can learn. It is a natural occurrence that happens when God wills it. All that we may do is prepare for this enlightenment by mastering our passions and accepting whatever fate may bring us. For a man with vision, all things are good, even if other people see them as evil. His knowledge of God gives him the ability to see Goodness at work even when he is mistreated by others. Those who are reborn are already living in the kingdom of heaven.

R e b i r t h

No one can be saved,
until he is born again.
If you want to be reborn,
purify yourself
of the irrational torments of matter.
The first of these is ignorance.
The second is grief.
Third is lack of self-control.
Fourth is desire.
Fifth is injustice.
Sixth is greed.
Seventh is deceit.
Eighth is envy.
Ninth is treachery.
Tenth is anger.
Eleventh is rashness.
Twelfth is malice.
Under these twelve are many more,
which force the man who is bound
to the prison of the body
to suffer from the torments they inflict.
But by Atum's mercy,
they may all depart
and be replaced by understanding.
This is the nature of rebirth.

This is the only road to reality.
It is the way our ancestors trod
to discover Primal Goodness.
It is sacred and divine,
but a hard highway for the soul
to travel in a body.
For the soul's first step
is to struggle against itself –
stirring up a civil war.
It is a feud of unity against duality.
The one seeking to unite
and the other seeking to divide.

He who is reborn
communes with the All-Father
who is Light and Life.
You will only experience this supreme vision
when you stop talking about it,
for this knowledge is deep silence
and tranquillity of the senses.
He who knows
the beauty of Primal Goodness
perceives nothing else.
He doesn't listen to anything.
He cannot move his body at all.
He forgets all physical sensations
and is still,
while the beauty of Goodness
bathes his mind in Light
and draws his soul out of his body –
making him One with eternal Being.
For a man cannot become a god
whilst he believes he is a body.
To become divine
he must be transformed
by the beauty of Primal Goodness.

The womb of rebirth is wisdom.
The conception is silence.
The seed is Goodness.
Those born of this birth
are not the same.
They are of the gods
and children of Atum – the One-God.
They contain all.
They are in all.
They are not made up of matter.
They are All-Mind.

Rebirth is not a theory
that you can strive to learn.
But when Atum wills,
he will re-Mind you.
A man may only seek to know Atum
by controlling his passions
and letting Destiny deal as she wills
with his body,
which is no more than clay
that belongs to Nature and not to him.
He should not attempt
to improve his life by magic
or oppose his fate using force,
but allow Necessity to follow its course.

For the man of vision,
all things are good,
even if they appear evil to others.
When men devise mischief against him,
he sees it in the light
of his knowledge of Atum,
and he –
and only he –
transforms evil into Goodness.

XIX. Secret Teachings

In this chapter Hermes reviews his teachings and encourages us to go beyond his words to a profound realisation of their truth.

The teachings of the ancient mystery religions were closely guarded secrets. An oath of secrecy, punishable by death, was taken by all initiates. In reality however, these secrets guard themselves. They are 'sacred open secrets' written in the language of nature, in the movement of the stars and the singing of the birds. The answers are there for all who are able to look and listen with minds unclouded by others' opinions.

Hermes has taught us some of these profound secrets. If we are not ready to receive them, we will simply not understand what we have read. Words lead us to the doorway of Truth, but only by contemplating their meaning can we pass through. If we meditate on these teachings we will know them to be true. If we don't, they will be just more concepts and opinions.

Hermes has tried to paint a picture of God for us. If we can catch his vision, it will take possession of our soul and lead us to Knowledge. It is hard to let go of our familiar way of seeing things but, by God's grace, we can be spiritually reborn and return to our original home.

God is like a musician who creates the harmonies of the Cosmos and gives each individual his own particular theme to play. If the music of life seems discordant to us, we should not blame the Master Musician, but ourselves. We are the out-of-tune instrument which mars the beauty of his composition.

Hermes reflects that when we devote ourselves to the spiritual path, we mysteriously become perfectly tuned. Hermes is aware of his own personal weaknesses, but God still makes him a perfect vehicle for his divine will, and can do the same for us if we are prepared to let him.

Secret Teachings

Now that you have learnt these secrets,
you must promise to keep silence
and never to reveal
how the rebirth is transmitted.
These teachings
have been set down in private
to be read only by those
whom Atum himself wills to know them.

Only if you contemplate
all that I have said
will you know it to be true.
If you do not –
you will not believe me.
For belief grows from contemplation,
and disbelief from lack of thought.
Speech alone cannot convey the Truth,
but the power of Mind is extraordinary,
and when it has been led by speech
to think things through thoroughly,
it can find the peace of true beliefs.
Only if grasped by thought, in this way,
will my teachings be understood.

I have, as far as is possible,
painted for you a likeness of Atum,

which if gazed upon
with the eyes of your heart
will lead you to the upward path.
The vision itself will be your guide,
for it has this power,
peculiar to itself,
that it takes possession
of those who have seen it
and draws them out,
just as a magnet draws iron
from the black earth.

This is the journey of Knowledge.
Speed towards this Knowledge,
for although it is hard
to let go of the familiar
and return to the old home
from which we originated,
Atum's grace never fails
and there is no end to his bounty.
He is by nature a musician
who composes the harmony of the Cosmos
and transmits to each individual
the rhythm of their own music.
If the music becomes discordant,
don't blame the musician,
but the lyre-string he plays,
that has become loose and sounds flat,
marring the perfect beauty of the melody.

But I have noticed
that when an artist
deals with a noble theme
his lyre becomes mysteriously tuned,
so that its deficiencies
issue glorious music,
to the amazement of his listeners.
It has been like this with me.
I confess my weaknesses,
but by Atum's power
my music is made good,
and he will likewise
make your music perfect.

There is no discord
amongst the inhabitants of heaven.
All have one purpose,
one mind, one feeling –
for they are bound by the spell of love
into one harmonious whole.
The earthly part of the universe
would seem rude and savage
without sweet melodies.
This is why Atum sent down
the choir of muses
to live amongst humankind
and inspire music,
so that men could adore Divinity
with hymns of praise,
in polyphony with the psalms of heaven.
So, let us adore Atum with deep gratitude
because words are only praise
when he accepts them.

XX. In Praise of Atum

**In this final chapter Hermes offers
up a glorious hymn to God.**

Through his teachings, Hermes has led us to the threshold
of Truth. All that he may do now is show us, by his own
example, the joy and liberation of crossing over. He aban-
dons himself in ecstatic rapture to a personal experience of
God. He sings the praises of God who is One and All; who
loves us like a Father and is the Mother of everything; the
eternal constancy which causes the whole universe to
change; the Goodness all around us. We can only thank
God for his many blessings by learning to know his greatness.

Yet Hermes knows it is God who is singing these
psalms through him. God is all that we do; all that we say;
all that we are; all that happens. Hermes has become a pas-
sive instrument of God's will. He no longer sees the world
with physical eyes, but witnesses the unfolding changes of
life within God's eternal Mind. He is no longer a body. He is
All-Mind. He is the presence which is present everywhere in
everything. He knows the One.

Hermes is overcome with mystical vision and realises
that, while still in the body, he has been made a god. He
prays for nothing, except that he will remain forever knowing and loving God. He is born again, and language is inadequate to express the wonders that he is experiencing. Like
the gods, he can now only sing God's praises through
silence.

In Praise of Atum

In a place open to the sky,
facing west at the hour of sunset
or east at sunrise,
I pray that the Cosmos be flung open to me
and that all nature
may receive the sound of my psalms.
Open, great earth,
and trees, silence your waving boughs,
for I am about to sing
the praise of the One and All.
Justice, praise the just through me.
Goodness, praise the good through me.
Truth, praise the true through me.
Selflessness, praise the All through me.
It is your words
that through me sing your praises –
for all comes from you
and all returns to you.
Accept these pure offerings of speech
from a heart and soul uplifted.
You of whom no words can tell,
no tongue can speak,
and only silence can declare.

I thank you with a brimming heart,
for it is only by your grace
that I see your Light
and come to know you.
I thank you whose name
no man knows.
You whom we honour
with the title 'Atum',
because you are our master.
You whom we call 'Father',
because you have shown
in all your acts towards us
the loving kindness and warm affection
that a father feels.
No – your love is greater
than a father's love,
for you have given us the gifts
of Mind and speech and Knowledge.
Mind, so that we may approach you.
Speech, that we may call to you.
Knowledge, so that we may experience you –
finding our salvation in your Light
and becoming filled with bliss.

We can thank you only by learning
to know your greatness.
I have learnt to know you.
You – the most brightly blazing Light of Mind.
I have learnt to know you.
You – the true Life of humankind.
I have learnt to know you.
You – the prolific all-womb
which impregnates itself.
I have learnt to know you.

In Praise of Atum

You – the eternal constancy
which stands unmoved,
and causes the whole universe
to revolve.

Who can speak about you?
Who can speak to you?
Where shall I look to praise you –
upwards or downwards?
For you are space
in which all things are contained.
There is no place but you.
All is in you.
What offering can I bring you?
For you are all things.
You give everything
and receive nothing.
There is nothing that you lack.
For what shall I praise you?
For the things you manifest,
or the things you conceal?
How shall I sing to you?
Am I my own?
Have I anything which is mine?
Am I other than you?
You are all that I am.
You are all that I do.
You are all that I say.
You are all that happens.
You are all that has not occurred.
You are Mind in your thinking.
You are Father in your creating.
You are Atum who does everything.
You are Primal Goodness everywhere.

You have revealed your Being,
and I am overcome.
While I am still in the body,
you have made me a god
by the gift of your eternal Life,
and I am filled with joy.
With these words of praise I adore you
who alone are Goodness.
I make no prayer but this –
that by your will,
I be kept always
still knowing and loving you,
and that I never fall away
from this blessed life.

Father, you have filled me
with this good and beautiful vision.
My mind's eye
is almost blinded with splendour,
more penetrating than visible light,
yet so full of immortal Life,
that it does not hurt or harm me.
By your mercy,
a form has been fashioned within me
which is not made of matter
and I have entered into an immortal body.
I have been born again in Mind
and the bodily shape
I had before has left me.
I am no longer an object –
tangible, coloured,
with spatial dimensions.
I am alien to all that is seen
with bodily eyesight.
To such eyes,
I am no longer visible.

In Praise of Atum

I am your instrument.
Mind is your plectrum,
and your wisdom plucks music from me.
I sing a song of my soul,
for your love has reached me.
You have made me a new being,
and I no longer see with bodily eyes
but witness with Mind.
When a man is born again
he is not a body of three dimensions.
He is All-Mind.
Now that I see in Mind
I perceive myself to be the All.
I am in heaven and earth.
I am in water and air.
I am in beasts and plants.
I am a new-born babe.
I am still in the womb.
I am yet to be conceived.
I am the presence which is present
everywhere.

I see incredible depths.
How can I describe this vision?
With my mind I see Mind.
I know the One
that wakes me from forgetfulness.
I see my soul.
I am afraid to speak.
I have found the source
of the power of all powers
that has no beginning.
I see a fountain bubbling with Life.

I am Mind!
I have seen!
I have found that which I seek.
I know peace in your purpose.
By your will,
I am born again.

Language is inadequate.
The gods sing a hymn of silence,
and I am silently singing.

Sources for Text

The text is compiled from the following writings which can be found in most versions of *The Hermetica*.

The Stobaeus. An anthology of Hermetic excerpts compiled by the scholar John of Stobae in the 5th century.

The Asclepius. Dialogue between Hermes and his son, usually printed as the first of the Hermetic books.

Books 1–18. The standard Corpus Hermeticum, not including Book 15.

Fragments. Important Hermetic fragments collected from the writings of many ancient authors, their number varies from edition to edition.

Nag Hammadi Hermetic Texts. New Hermetic material discovered amongst the Gnostic gospels found in Nag Hammadi in 1945.

I. **The Prophecies of Hermes**
The Asclepius; the Stobaeus; the Nag Hammadi Hermetic texts

II. **The Initiation of Hermes**
The Asclepius; the Nag Hammadi Hermetic texts; fragments; the Corpus Hermeticum, Books 1 and 3

III. **The Being of Atum**
The Asclepius; the Stobaeus; the Corpus Hermeticum, Books 2, 4, 6, 9, 12, 13, 14 and 16

IV. **Contemplate Creation**
The Stobaeus; the Corpus Hermeticum, Books 5, 9, 12 and 14

V. **The Living Cosmos**
The Asclepius; the Stobaeus; the Corpus Hermeticum, Books 1, 4, 8, 10, 12 and 17

VI. **The Circle of Time**
The Asclepius; the Stobaeus

VII. **The Gods**
The Asclepius; the Stobaeus; the Corpus Hermeticum, Books 1, 10 and 16

Further Reading

Armstrong, Karen, *The History of God*, London. 1993

Burkert, Walter, *Greek Religion*, Blackwell, Oxford. 1985

Cronin, Vincent, *The Florentine Renaissance*, Collins, London. 1967

French, Peter, *John Dee – The World of an Elizabethan Magus*, Routledge, London. 1972

Guthrie, Kenneth, *The Pythagorean Sourcebook and Library*, Phanes Press, USA. 1987

Kingsley, Peter, *Ancient Philosophy, Mystery and Magic*, Clarendon Press, Oxford. 1995

Lamy, Lucy, *The Mysteries of Ancient Egypt*, Thames & Hudson, London. 1981.

Yates, Frances, *Giordano Bruno and Hermetic Tradition*, University of Chicago Press, USA. 1964

Yates, Frances, *The Rosicrucian Enlightenment*, Routledge, London. 1972

About the Authors

Timothy Freke has an honours degree in philosophy and has been a lifelong student of world spiritual thought and practice. He has travelled extensively, and has been instructed by masters from many different traditions. He is the author of many books on mystical philosophy including *The Tao Te Ching* (Piatkus 1995) and with Peter Gandy *The Complete Guide to World Mysticism* (Piatkus 1997).

Peter Gandy is a researcher into the roots of the Western mystery tradition, with a comprehensive understanding of ancient texts and contemporary commentaries. He is currently reading for an M.A. in Classical Civilisation at Birkbeck College, London. He has spent many years studying the philosophy of Hermes Trismegistus and its impact on the history of modern culture.